I0792937

Historic Tales *of* SENECA COUNTY NEW YORK

WALTER GABLE

THE History PRESS

Published by The History Press
Charleston, SC
www.historypress.net

Front cover, top: Seneca County Historian's Office; *bottom*: Seneca Falls Historical Society.
Back cover: Walter Gable; *insert*: Walter Gable.

First published 2017

Manufactured in the United States

ISBN 9781467136549

Library of Congress Control Number: 2017934928

Notice: The information in this book is true and complete to the best of our knowledge. It is offered without guarantee on the part of the author or The History Press. The author and The History Press disclaim all liability in connection with the use of this book.

Contents

CONTENTS

Acknowledgements

This book has become a reality thanks to the assistance and support of many people. The constant encouragement and help from close friends and local historians has sustained me in this endeavor. I mention these in particular: Naomi Brewer, Carolyn Zogg, Philomena Cammuso, Bill Sebring, Allan Buddle, Jane Braunig and Gail Snyder.

This is my third book published by The History Press. Looking back now, I realize how much patience its extremely professional staff had as they guided me through the learning curves of completing my first book, *The Seneca Army Depot: Fighting Wars from the New York Home Front*. Their expertise and my enhanced understanding of the process made publication of the second book, *Seneca County and the Civil War*, much easier. Amanda Irle, Rick Delaney and the other staff have made my work on this third book pleasant and almost routine. I am grateful and thankful for that.

The Seneca County Board of Supervisors and several members of the county staff have been instrumental in making my work as the Seneca County historian possible and so enjoyable. Their support is greatly appreciated. They have given me much freedom to choose what topics I pursue for my writing and program presentations.

The late Miss Ethel M. Buckley, my high school history teacher, instilled in me a great love of history. In much of my writing, I am guided by asking myself if Miss Buckley would think my wording is appropriate and would pass the test of being factually correct.

Introduction

I took on the part-time position of Seneca County historian in August 2003, because it was just too intriguing a challenge and opportunity to pass up. I transformed the job, placing emphases on writing about Seneca County's rich history and presenting programs to schools and community groups. Much of my time was spent on research and writing.

My extensive writing reached a larger audience when it began appearing as articles in local newspapers. The *Reveille/Between the Lakes*, a weekly publication and one of the official newspapers of county government, began running an article of my choice on a monthly basis. Starting in 2009, I was also producing articles every week for the *Tri-Village Pennysaver* and every four weeks for the *Finger Lakes Times*.

It is very typical that, almost anywhere I go locally, someone comes up to me and expresses how much they have enjoyed reading my articles. Several people tell me that they save them. I have also been asked by many people if I am going to compile them into a book. After writing two books rather specific in content for The History Press—*The Seneca Army Depot: Fighting Wars from the New York Home Front* and *Seneca County and the Civil War*—I decided that it was time to do a book covering many of the topics about which I have written as the Seneca County historian. These topics include histories of important individuals, businesses and events. They are presented here in no order of chronology or significance. This assortment of topics is reflected in the book title—*Historic Tales of Seneca County, New York*.

In preparing this book, it was difficult to determine which articles to include and which not to include. I have written on so many topics that I could do several volumes of *Historic Tales of Seneca County, New York*. Some of this book's chapters cover topics about which I have written for local newspapers. Unlike the newspaper versions, however, the chapters on those topics in this book are unabridged and have source citations.

The first two chapters in this book were obvious choices from a historical standpoint. The first chapter deals with the establishment of Seneca County and its towns. One section of the chapter, "Encounters with Wild Animals in the Early 1800s," gives the reader some idea of just how much of a frontier this area was at the time. Another section, "History of the Formation of the Various Towns," is especially helpful for readers to understand the changes in the boundary lines of the various towns and of the county as a whole. I frequently get genealogical requests from people who are seeking information about some ancestor, along the lines that some person was believed to be living in one town, then moved to another town and then to still another. But, in many cases, the person didn't move at all! For example, someone living in Romulus in 1794 might not have to move to be recorded as living in the town of Washington in 1803. They might then be documented as living in the town of Junius in 1804, then in Seneca Falls in 1830. Another possibility is that a person living in Romulus in 1794 would, without having moved, be recorded as living in Wayne County in 1824. Such "movements" were the product of shifting boundary lines as counties were established and altered.

The second chapter deals with the official county seal. Although it is the shortest chapter in the book, it touches on several aspects of the county's history. My book *Seneca County and the Civil War* devotes full chapters to the Scythe Tree story and to Waterloo as the official birthplace of Memorial Day.

The chapter dealing with Ezra Sutton, who hit the first home run in professional major-league baseball, is the result of some of my most recent research and writing. On January 25, 2016, I was presenting a program on the Seneca Army Depot book at the Galen Historical Society in Clyde, New York. At the conclusion of the program, Jim Darnell asked me what I knew about a baseball player, Ezra Sutton, who was born in Seneca Falls. I didn't even recognize the name, but I soon got to work, researching as much as I could about Sutton. The Internet is such a helpful tool! I even purchased prints of baseball cards of Ezra Sutton. When I found out that he was buried in a cemetery in Palmyra, New York, I contacted Beth Hoad, the Palmyra town historian. She didn't know about Sutton but agreed to take a picture of his gravestone for me. She went on to write an article about Sutton for her series on local history in a Wayne County newspaper. Sutton's 1880 contract with the Boston team "came up missing" from the New York Public Library and then appeared in a collector's auction at Sotheby's. I have been unable to verify the current location of that contract, so the chapter does not deal with that controversy.

Many of the chapters touch on favorite topics of mine. In my youth, I was fascinated to see the blades of the Windmill turn and to hear stories about the Kingdom community. I have always been fascinated by cobblestone houses, so it should not be surprising that one of my earliest extensive research efforts as county historian was to start compiling information about the cobblestone houses in Seneca County. The recent movie version of the book *In the Heart of the Sea* only heightened my interest in the tale of a whale story.

I hope that you enjoy this book and that it gives you insight into the rich history of Seneca County. It may be one of the smaller counties in New York State, but it has great history. The county is the site of the birth of the women's rights movement, is the official birthplace of Memorial Day and was home to the former Seneca Army Depot. And Seneca County is home to lots of other interesting stories. My part-time job has continued to be a full-time hobby.

1

Establishment of Seneca County and Its Towns

Origins of Seneca County

Prior to March 24, 1804, today's Seneca County was part of various counties. When counties were established in New York State in 1683, the present-day Seneca County was part of the vast Albany County. A portion of Albany County became Tryon County on March 12, 1772. This county was named for William Tryon, colonial governor of New York. In 1784, following the peace treaty that ended the Revolutionary War, Tryon County was renamed Montgomery County in honor of the American general Richard Montgomery. On February 16, 1791, portions of Montgomery County became Tioga, Otsego and Herkimer Counties. Onondaga County was established from a portion of Herkimer County on March 5, 1794. The western portion of Onondaga County became Cayuga County on March 8, 1799. At that time, Cayuga County included the present Seneca and Tompkins Counties and part of Wayne County.

Seneca County was established from the western part of Cayuga County by an act passed by the New York State legislature on March 24, 1804. At that time, Seneca County stretched all the way from Lake Ontario to what is today Ithaca. More specifically, it was bounded on the north by Lake Ontario, on the east by Cayuga County, on the south by Tioga County and on the west by Steuben and Ontario Counties. It was a strip some 63 miles

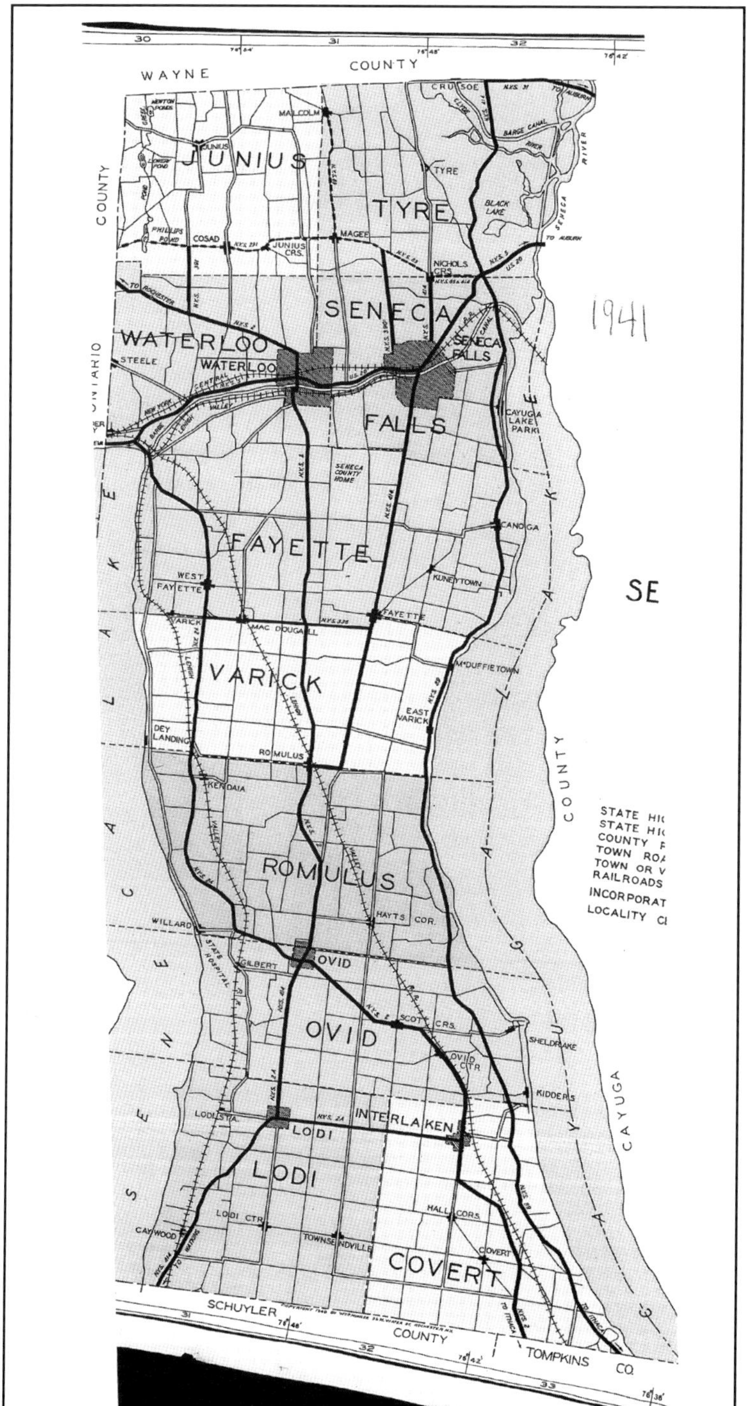
WAYNE
COUNTY
JUNIUS
TYRE
SENECA
WATERLOO
SENECA FALLS
FAYETTE
VARICK
ROMULUS
OVID
LODI
COVERT
INTERLAKEN
1941
SCHUYLER
COUNTY
TOMPKINS CO.
ONTARIO COUNTY
CAYUGA COUNTY
SENECA LAKE
CAYUGA LAKE

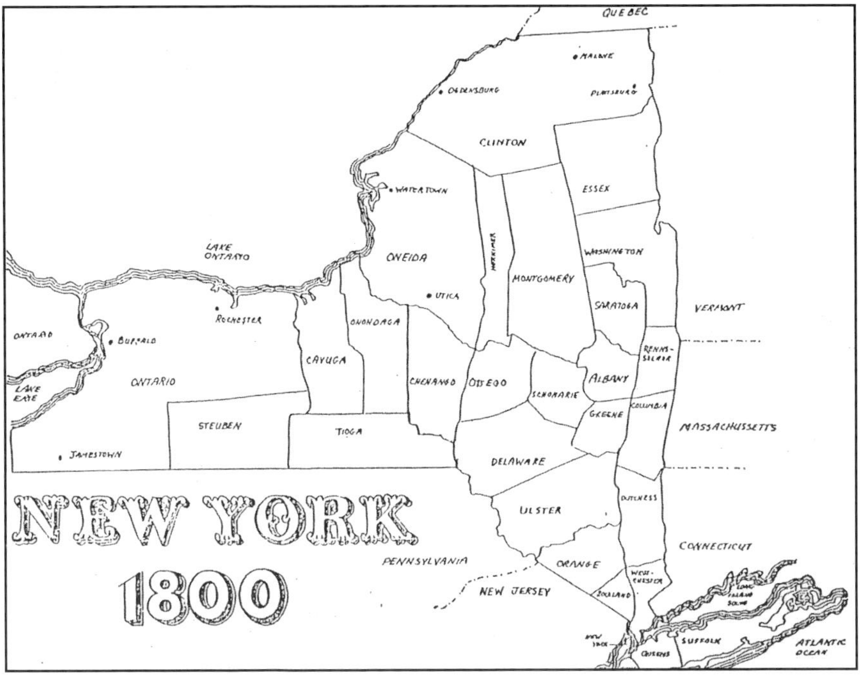

Above: Present-day Seneca County was the western part of Cayuga County in 1800. *Seneca County Historian's Office.*

Opposite: Seneca County consists of ten towns and is referred to as the "County Between the Lakes." *Seneca County Historian's Office.*

in length with an average width of 11 miles, totaling 744 square miles, or about half a million acres.

Encounters with Wild Animals in the Early 1800s

The 1876 Everts history of Seneca County (pages 31–32) provides true stories of early residents' encounters with wild animals—something we rarely have to consider today.

The first of these stories, occurring about 1800, involves young men hunting on Crusoe Island, located near the northeast corner of present-day Seneca County.

> *A boat-load of young men went to hunt deer upon Crusoe Island. The boat left them, to return in a week. Wolves, numerous and hungry, had driven off the deer. One of the youths went out alone in quest of game. A large black bear was seen upon a chestnut-tree, but disappeared before the hunter reached the spot. He shot and dressed a squirrel, and then set out for camp. It grew dark, and the silence was broken by the prolonged howl of a distant wolf. Here and there an echoing howl replied, and soon a pack had gathered where he had killed the squirrel, and then he knew they were following on his track. He reached and passed a spot where "Indian John"* [who was hanged for the murder of Ezekiel Crane] *had battled with just such a pack all night. With clubbed rifle he had struck the nearest as their white fangs snapped at him. Morning had come, and the Indian, with torn arms, shattered gun, and dead wolves around him, had seen the pack leave with infinite relief; yet here the white boy was hurrying on and looking for a tree to climb, when the report of a signal gun from camp renewed his courage. The wolves came nearer, and at the discharge of his rifle stopped silent for a moment. Reloading, he hastened on, and again checked pursuit by firing; a third shot was delivered close to camp, the wolves upon his heels. Driven off, the pack continued howling around the fires until daybreak dispersed them in the woods.*[1]

Although we still have many squirrels around, they were clearly more numerous in the early 1800s, as evidenced by the following anecdote: "Squirrels were so numerous, and depredated so upon the crops, that the settlers formed in companies, headed by their best marksmen, and gave a day to hunting them. Two thousand squirrels were slain at a single hunt. After the sport, came supper and spirits at some log tavern, the bill being paid by the side having least scalps."[2]

Young lads had to learn early on how to use a gun, as illustrated in this 1805 story about an encounter with a panther:

> *In the year 1805, or thereabouts, a boy of sixteen…heard his dog barking in the woods about half a mile distant, and purposed to go and see what he had there. It was about nine o'clock and the night was very dark; the mother objected to his going, as her husband was away at the time. The boy gained his point and set off with gun and axe, accompanied by his younger brother, carrying a lighted torch of hickory-bark. The dog barked louder as the light drew near. Pushing their way through a thicket, they found there was something concealed in the thick leaves and*

> *branches of a large tree-top. While the younger boy held the torch, the elder, creeping under the top from the opposite side, groped his way up to some animal which turned towards him, and then to the dog, which had come closer. The glimmer of the light gave to it a white appearance, and the boys, concluding it was a stray sheep, called off the dog and went home. The father discredited the idea of a sheep, and next day saw signs of some animal and tracks of the dog, but no sheep. One day, some weeks later, father and son were seated upon a log, resting from their work of getting out timber, and eating their luncheon, part of which was roast venison, when their dog, growling, crouched at their feet. Set on, he bounded forward with a bark, and back and tail of an animal were seen as it leaped away through the brush. The father, turning pale, exclaimed, "My God! what a panther!" The panther prowled about the house all night. The father being called away on a journey, the boy determined to try a shot at the wild beast during his absence. The gun was cleaned and loaded with two balls, and John Updike and brother invited to come over and help "top" turnips and bring their "bear" dog. Night came; the dog was left out-doors, a torch made ready to light, and turnip-topping began. Presently the large dog in the house began to growl, and the dog outside was heard loudly barking. The torch was lighted, the boy stole out, and some eight rods off saw the panther's glaring eyes fixed upon the house. Gun in hand at the corner of the house, the boy could presently see the dark form outlined by the torchlight held by John Updike, while by him his brother William held their dog. The gun was aimed between the panther's eyes, the trigger pulled, and the gun flashed. The torch fell, the dogs sprang out and seized the animal as he bounded upon his assailant. The Updike boys rushed into the house and closed the door. The panther's paw struck close to the youth as the dogs caught and held him. Successive blows laid out the wounded animal, and the fierce panther escaped to the woods and troubled them no more.*[3]

SUBSEQUENT BOUNDARY CHANGES TO SENECA COUNTY

The southwestern portion of the town of Ovid was taken away on March 30, 1802, to become part of the town of Hector. On April 7, 1817, Ovid was divided, the southern portion becoming the town of Covert. On that same day, the town of Covert was taken away from Seneca County and became part of Tompkins County. The former town of Covert was returned to Seneca County on April 13, 1819.

The northern portions of Seneca County (the towns of Galen and Wolcott) were taken away from Seneca County on April 11, 1823, to become parts of the newly created Wayne County. At this point, Seneca County totaled about 197,500 acres of land.

HISTORY OF THE FORMATION OF THE VARIOUS TOWNS

At the time of Seneca County's creation, on March 24, 1804, it consisted of the towns of Ovid, Romulus, Washington and Junius. Ovid and Romulus had been established on March 5, 1794. The town of Washington was formed from the northern portion of Romulus on March 14, 1800. Junius was created from the northern portion of Washington on February 12, 1803.

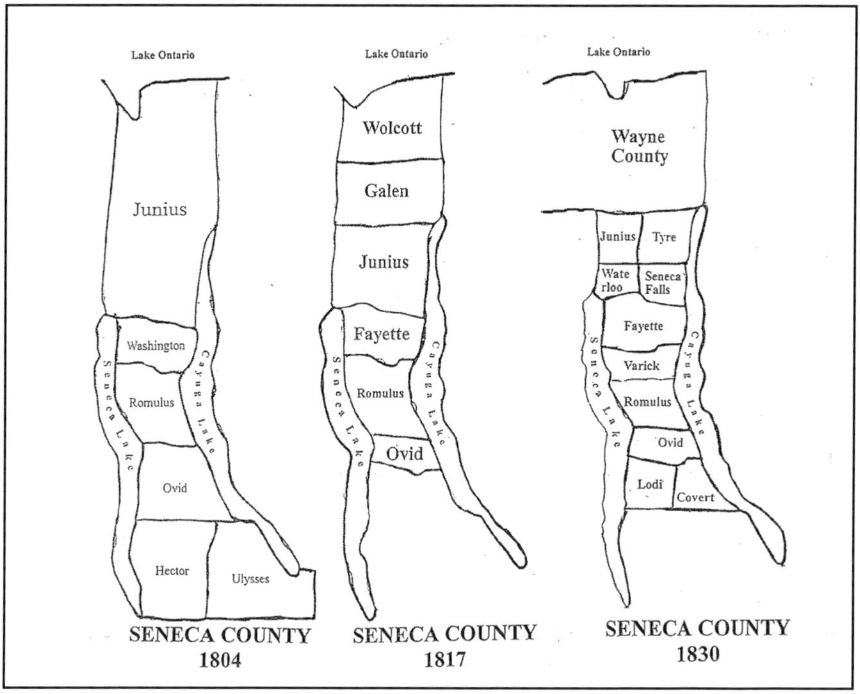

The boundaries of Seneca County itself, as well as the various towns of the county, have changed greatly since 1804. *Seneca County Historian's Office.*

The town of Washington was renamed Fayette on April 6, 1808. This change was made by the New York State legislature to avoid confusing this portion of Seneca County with the town of Washington in Dutchess County, which had been organized by the legislature on March 13, 1786. Virtually everyone at the time remembered the crucial contributions that General Gilbert Motier de LaFayette, the beloved companion-in-arms to General George Washington, had made during the American Revolution.[4]

Covert was formed from the southern portion of the town of Ovid on April 7, 1817. On March 30, 1843, Lots 34, 40, 41 and 42 of Military Tract Township No. 16 (Ovid) were transferred from the town of Ovid to the town of Covert.

The town of Lodi was formed from the western portion of Covert on January 27, 1826. On May 5, 1837, the north line of the town was advanced one mile with the annexation of Military Lots 26, 35, 36, 37, 38 and 39 from the town of Ovid.

The towns of Seneca Falls, Tyre and Waterloo were formed from portions of Junius on March 26, 1829.

The town of Varick was formed from the northern portion of Romulus on February 6, 1830.

2

The Official County Seal for Seneca County, New York

The official seal for Seneca County, New York, was formally adopted by the board of supervisors on July 22, 1975. The former county seal had been just a plain white circle with the words "County of Seneca, New York" and a star around the edge with the word "Seal" in the center. The new county seal was in color and included several images that referred to important aspects of the rich history of Seneca County. How this new county seal came about is described by Sharon Secor, who was deputy clerk of the board of supervisors at the time. Secor said, "The Board of Supervisors had decided that it was time to update the County Seal to reflect actual representation of the county and its history. So a contest was held, not just limited to school kids, but open to anyone. A committee was formed to select one that was representative of the county and its history and present it to the Board."[5] The adopted design was actually a composite of a few submitted entries, with some changes made.

The elements on the seal represent the following corresponding aspects of the county and its history:

Indian head: Indian heritage
Vote 1848: the Seneca Falls Women's Rights Convention of July 19–20
Scythe 1861: the Scythe Tree, on which James Wyman Johnson hung his scythe, near his house, and tells his parents he is going to enlist in the Union army
Flag 1866: the first Memorial Day celebration in Waterloo

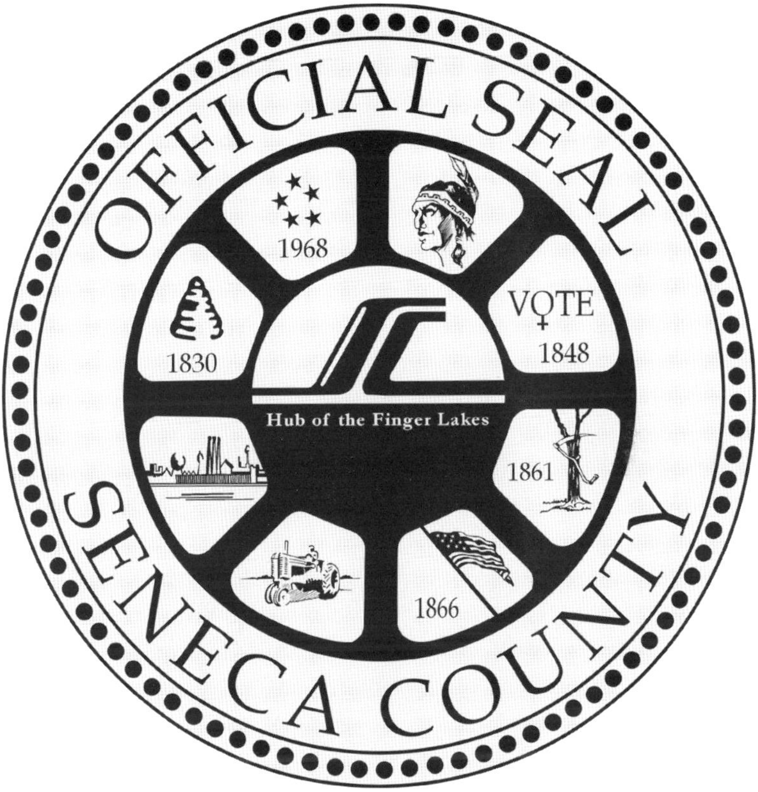

The official Seneca County seal includes various images reflecting different aspects of the county's rich history. *Seneca County IT Department.*

Tractor: agriculture
Buildings in skyline: industry
Beehive 1830: establishment of the Church of Jesus Christ of Latter-day Saints (Mormon Church) by Joseph Smith; the Mormons later settled in Utah, which has the nickname the Beehive State
Five stars 1968: establishment of Eisenhower College (Dwight Eisenhower was a five-star general)

The stylized letters *S* and *C* in the center stand for "Seneca County." Their form also represents waves, depicting the two lakes that bound the county on the east and the west.[6]

3

The New York State College of Agriculture at Ovid (Willard)

Before the Willard Asylum for the Insane was established, the site was the New York State Agricultural College, the first state-chartered agricultural college in New York. As early as 1842, the New York Agricultural Society had been urging the creation of agricultural schools or colleges. Many European countries had already established colleges of agriculture to help train farmers to make better use of the new farming methods and technology developing as part of the Industrial Revolution.

In 1851, John Delafield of Fayette became president of the New York Agricultural Society and made it a priority to get the legislature to create an agricultural college. On April 1, 1853, Chapter 247 of state laws incorporated the New York State Agricultural College. The college's trustees selected Oaklands farm in Fayette, the home of Delafield, as the site for the college. With Delafield's sudden death on October 22, however, nothing further was done for nearly two years.

In 1855, the idea of a state agricultural college was revived. Several communities—Ithaca, Aurora, Kings Ferry, Farmer (Interlaken), Sheldrake and Ovid—aspired to be chosen as the site. Ovid emerged victorious, largely due to the promotional efforts of the Reverend Amos Brown, principal of the Seneca Collegiate Institute in Ovid. He raised $46,000 locally and got the New York legislature to grant a $40,000 loan. Over six hundred acres were purchased in the towns of Ovid and Romulus near Seneca Lake, close to a tiny settlement called Baileytown (Ovid Landing). A large brick building was to be constructed to house students and provide classrooms for 350 students.

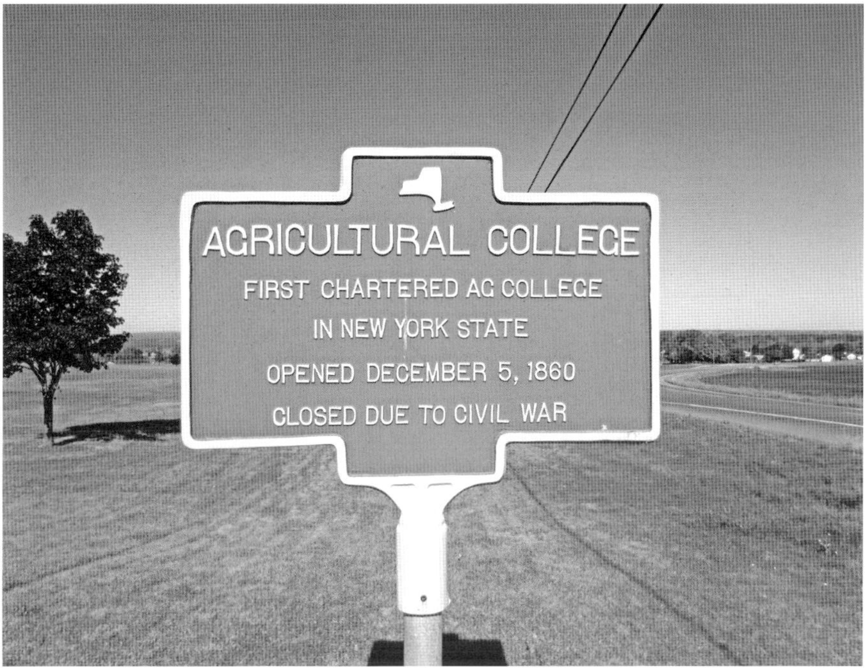

Above: In 2008, local historians erected a historic marker honoring the Agricultural College at Ovid. *Walter Gable.*

Right: John Delafield of Fayette was instrumental in securing from the New York State legislature a charter for the first state agricultural college. *Wayne E. Morrison Sr.*

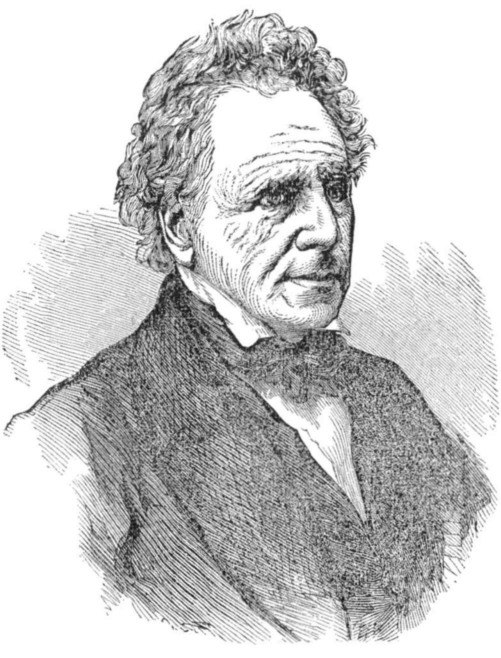

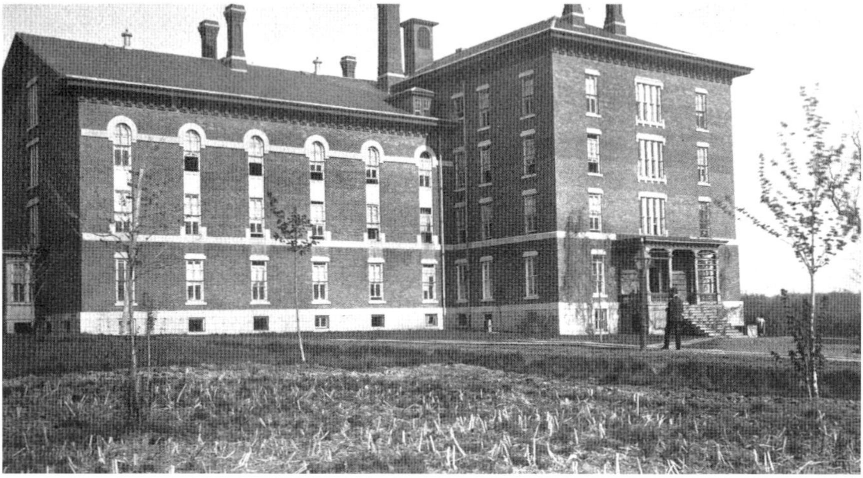

This was the agricultural college building when the college opened in December 1860. *Wayne E. Morrison Sr.*

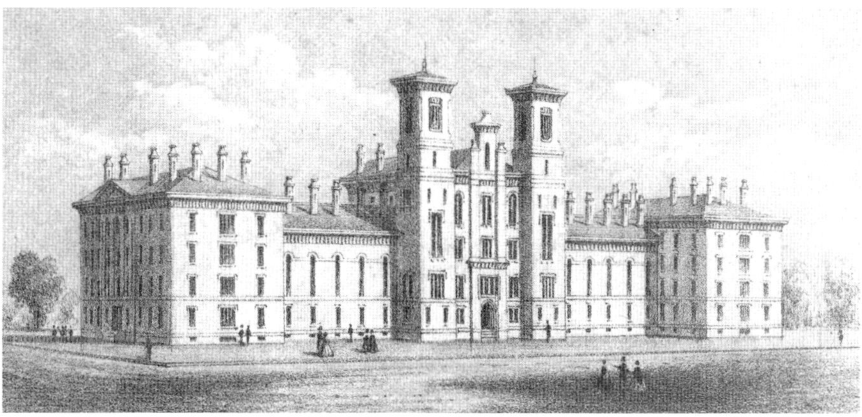

This was the original, envisioned agricultural college building, but only the small portion at right was actually constructed. *Wayne E. Morrison Sr.*

The college was opened on December 5, 1860. Major Marsena R. Patrick, a West Point graduate, was the president. For $200 a year, students received classroom instruction and on-the-farm experience to become familiar with "the principles and practice of the methods of clearing and cleaning land, nourishment of plants and grasses, restoration and exhaustion of the soil, rotation of crops and their adaptation to the season, gathering hay and grain, management of the dairy, gardening, fattening, rearing and breeding stock, training colts, the disease of animals and veterinary practice, preparation of timber for fences, surveying, landscape gardening and bookkeeping as applied to farming."[7]

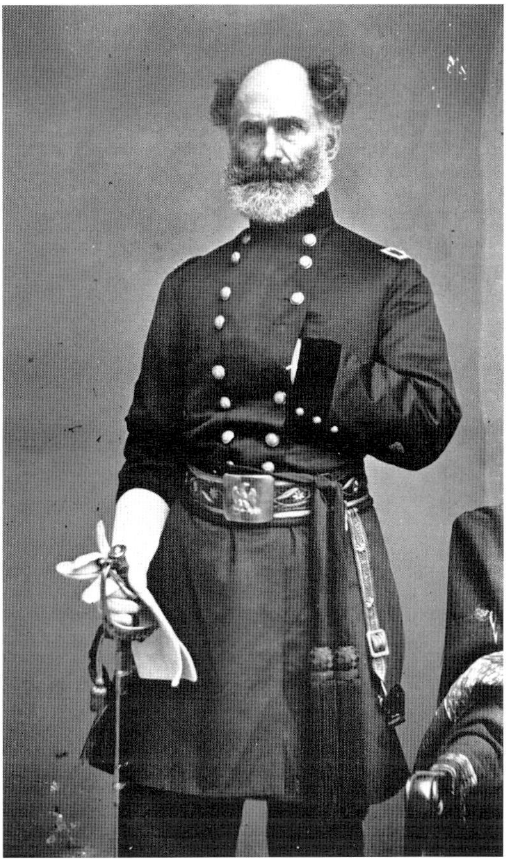

General Marsena R. Patrick was the president of the college, but he was called into military duty when the Civil War started. *Wayne E. Morrison Sr.*

The timing for the opening of this college was bad. Throughout the winter of 1860 and early 1861, there was constant talk of pending war. Within two weeks of the fall of Fort Sumter in April 1861, President Patrick was called to Albany by Governor Edwin Morgan. Patrick was to draw upon his previous army experience to devise a means for rapid enlistment and training of volunteers. Believing that the war would be of short duration, the college tried to carry on in Patrick's absence. By May, so many of the approximately forty students had left to fight that the college closed for the summer. It did not reopen in the fall or in the winter. In March 1862, it was officially announced that the "college doors are closed for the present." On August 9, about two hundred acres of the college's land were sold because of debts owed.

Although the Baileytown area's agricultural college was short-lived, there was soon a new state agricultural college in nearby Ithaca. Ezra Cornell, who in 1864 had started a university bearing his name, was determined that the school would include an agricultural college. This had been promised to him when the state granted its charter. To make the promise a reality, Cornell secured the services of Reverend Amos Brown to lobby in Albany and Washington, D.C., on behalf of Cornell University. The Republican-controlled Congress had passed one of a series of Morrill Acts in 1862, providing for what became known as "land grant" colleges in engineering, agriculture and military science. Reverend Brown was instrumental in convincing the New York State legislature to award New York's new land-grant agricultural college to Cornell University.[8] The school's emphasis on experience "in the field" became the model for all agricultural colleges' educational programs.

Soon, Ovid-area residents turned their energies to getting the former agricultural college site in Baileytown chosen as the location for a new state asylum. This became reality in October 1869, when the first patients were admitted to the new Willard Asylum for the Insane. The former agricultural college building was converted and opened in the summer of 1870 as the branch for two hundred female patients.[9]

In 1960, Governor Nelson Rockefeller helped dedicate a boulder with a plaque commemorating the 100th anniversary of the opening of the agricultural college at Ovid.

In September 1995, the Willard Drug Treatment Campus opened on most of the site of the former Willard Psychiatric State Hospital, which was the successor name to the original Willard Asylum for the Insane. The hospital closed in 1995.

On July 14, 2008, local historians presented a public program on the history of the New York State Agricultural College at Ovid. Several important state and local dignitaries spoke at that program, including Patrick Hooker, the New York State commissioner of agriculture, and Robert Weible, the New York State historian. At that program, the new historical marker was dedicated.

The agricultural college at what is today Willard was gone, but the Willard Asylum for the Insane would flourish for many years. The new state agricultural college at Cornell University thrives today.

4

Automobiles in Seneca County: Early History

Over one hundred years ago, the first Model T automobile was made. It was not the first car to be built, but it was the first widely affordable, mass-produced car. The first Model T went on sale on October 1, 1908, at a price of about $850. Between 1908 and 1927, a total of fifteen million Model Ts were sold. By the 1920s, half of all the cars in America were Model Ts. The 1925 Model T touring car cost about $260, at a time when the average annual income in America was $1,236.[10]

In January 1906, Dr. C.C. Bachman purchased the first automobile to be owned in Waterloo. His car was a fifteen-horsepower Pope that he purchased at an automobile show in New York City. In July of that same year, H.I. Buttery purchased a twenty-five-horsepower Pope Hartford automobile that he drove from Syracuse to Waterloo.[11]

Automobile Races through Waterloo

Automobiles, however, had been seen in Waterloo and Seneca County before 1906. John E. Becker in his *A History of the Village of Waterloo* states that the *Automobile Review* of August 13, 1904, gave an extended account of Frank A. LaRoche's 3,314-mile nonstop, round-trip run between New York City and St. Louis. In the account, LaRoche said the following: "Between Syracuse and Rochester, at Seneca Falls I think it was, I got stuck in the mud and it took me five hours of hard work to dig the machine out and get started again. My hands are covered with blisters from the work!" This incident is said to have happened just west of the Village of Seneca Falls and "illustrates one of the drawbacks to automobiling through the country." It was also reported just a few years later that the Village of Waterloo was "known from coast to coast" for having some of the worst streets over which automobiles had to pass in crossing the continent.[12]

Becker's *History* also reports that seventy-six automobiles came through Waterloo on July 11, 1906, as part of the 1906 Glidden Tour. This was the third annual run of the American Auto Association, covering a distance of 4,135 miles in sixteen days. The object of the race was to see which make of machines would last the longest and perform the best in terms of endurance and maintenance. Becker reported the following:

> *Main Street was lined with sightseers who were well repaid for "looking." It took the entire afternoon for the passage of the "Cars" through the village. Late in the forenoon came the pilot cars and finely cut strips of paper (called confetti) were thrown from them to mark the route, which through the business section was on the south side of the street. There were about 300 passengers in the whole number, of which fifteen were ladies. The latter wore the customary veiling, while the men were generally clad in long brown linen dusters with the regulation caps and goggles.*[13]

The Iroquois Car Company in Seneca Falls

According to a 1967 *Reveille* article written by June Callahan, what became the Peter Koch car dealership at 221–229 Fall Street in Seneca Falls was the site of the manufacture of the Iroquois automobile. The Iroquois Type D car was a thirty-five-horsepower touring car with a one-hundred-inch wheelbase. It was sold for $2,500. The Iroquois Type E was a forty-horsepower, seven-passenger car with four-and-a-half- by thirty-two-inch tires and platform springs on the rear, with a selling price of $3,000 FOB (freight on board) Seneca Falls.

John Kaiser was the president of the Iroquois Motor Car Company between 1903 and 1909. Only thirteen cars were actually built, but they were quality cars. The small number of vehicles produced was largely a result of Kaiser's approach to building automobiles—considerably different

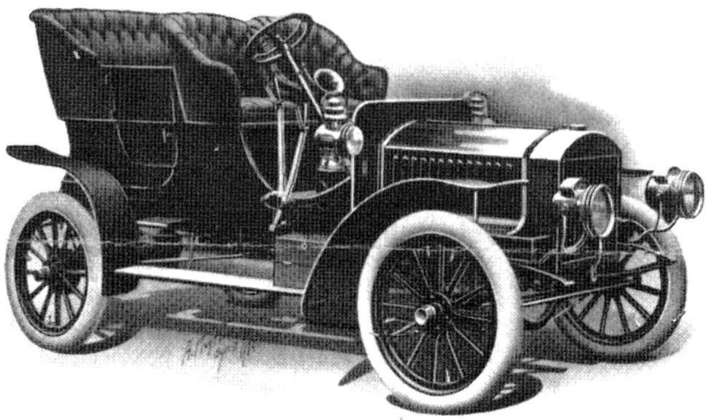

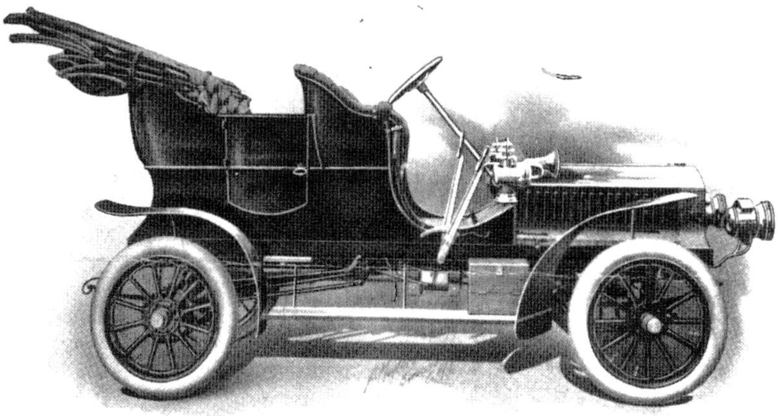

These are two models of Iroquois cars made in Seneca Falls. *National Automotive History Collection.*

from today's procedures. In a nod to the manufacturers of carriages, he built his cars to last. He considered a $3,000 automobile to be a very serious investment, and he expected his customers to drive his cars for twenty years or more. Because he wanted to build durability into his cars, he inspected and re-inspected every part, and he and his employees assembled the entire automobile. In 1909, the company dissolved because of lack of business. Callahan speculated in her article that "had Mr. Kaiser thought the same way as Henry Ford, maybe the Iroquois Motor would be a booming industry in Seneca Falls today."[14]

Automobiles in Seneca Falls

In the same article, Callahan reported that "the streets of Seneca Falls were traveled in the years that followed by many makes that are no longer in production." Residents owned many of these makes: Norman Gould owned an American Under-Slung; Fred Fisher owned a Winton; Walter Ward Sr. owned a Mora; Dr. Ernest F. Horton had an Overland; Charlie Fegley had an REO; Harry Fredenburg had a Franklin; Paul Perkins Sr. had a Saxon; W.E. Dickey had a Paige; and a Mrs. Partridge had a Pierce-Arrow.

The May 30, 1913 issue of the *Seneca Falls Reveille* noted that local residents had automobile fever. There were 89 Model Ts, plus a number of other car makes in the village. In January 1921, there were 2,073 autos and trucks in the county; by September of that year, the number had increased to 2,945. On October 27, 1922, Fred L. Huntington leased a building at Fall and Mynderse Streets for automobile sales.[15]

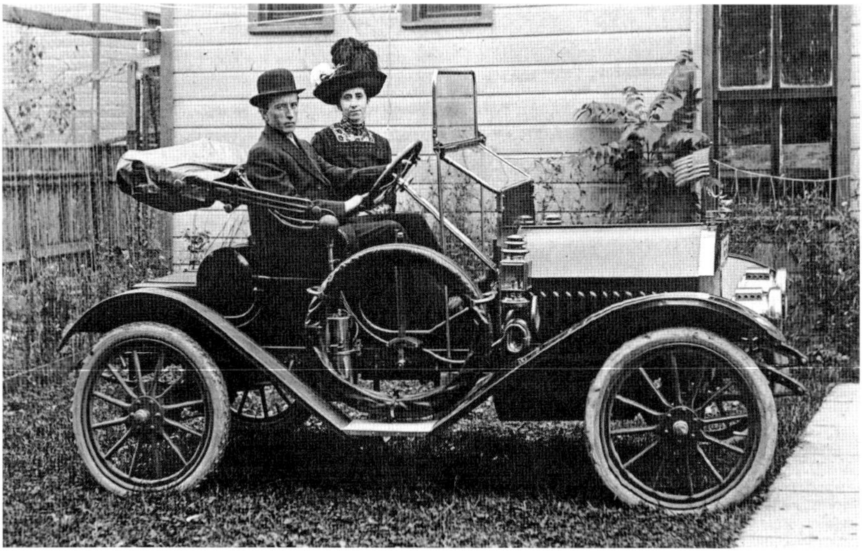

A couple enjoys an outing in Seneca Falls in their new car, circa 1915. *Seneca Falls Historical Society.*

Problems with Early Automobiles

In the early twentieth century, getting a car to start, especially after it stalled out, was not an easy task. Virtually everyone knows of the necessity of "cranking" the motor. Not everyone knows, however, of the "runaway automobile" incident of September 17, 1917, in Waterloo. Just as the crowd was dispersing from the New York Central Railroad station after seeing off a large contingent of Seneca County men who had entered the army for war duty, William Redfield's big Studebaker car became stalled at the main village intersection. When it wouldn't start, a number of helping hands gave it a push. The car was still in gear, and there was no driver in the seat. The runaway car struck another automobile and then took to the sidewalk, where it tore down awnings along the street. In front of Semtner's tailor shop, the car struck and killed H. Eugene Van Buren, who was repairing the sidewalk. The car then struck two little girls and then a tree in front of John C. Shanks's residence, on the corner of Church and Main Streets. The car bounded across the street and crashed into the house of Edward Conant, just east of the Presbyterian church. Becker summarized the incident this way: "Every part of the auto's driverless trip down the street was a freak occurrence."[16]

Ovid's 1903 Ford Model A

From about 1949 until the fall of 2014, a 1903 Ford Model A was on display at the N.R. Boyce car dealership in Ovid. The chain-driven car was often clogged with mud and other impediments.[17] The car, a first-year production, has an eight-horsepower 1903 Runabout. It was purchased in the fall of 2014 by Andrew Herrala, who soon sent it to RM Restorations in Canada to undergo major restoration work. Every piece of the car has been taken apart, evaluated, repaired as necessary and restored to its original condition. According to Herrala, "While just 56 of 677 Fords remain from 1903, this particular car is significantly original. The front seat still had the original leather upholstery, all the mechanical components were still intact. It does appear as though the car was involved in an accident many years ago that knocked the rear wheel from the axle and damaged a fender." The restored car will make its debut at the Amelia Island Concours in Florida in 2017.[18]

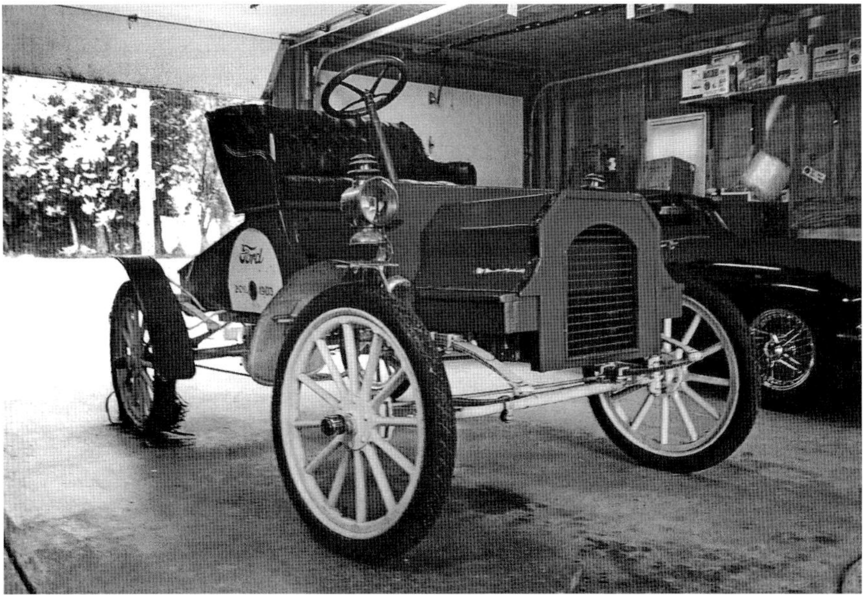

This two-cylinder 1903 Ford Model A was on public display for many years at the N.R. Boyce car showroom in Ovid. *Andy Herrala.*

To clarify why this model was labeled a Model A, early Ford cars were simply lettered Model A, then Model B and so on. The Model T proved so popular that Ford kept producing it for several years. Ford then went back to producing a new Model A.

AUTOMOBILES BROUGHT CHANGE

Area villages changed to accommodate the increase in automobile usage. Waterloo, for example, erected its first street signs in late 1910.[19] In June 1913, a five-year contract was made with Central New York and Electric Company for all-night street lighting in Waterloo. This lighting consisted of five ornamental cluster lamps of sixty candlepower each to be placed on each side of Main Street, one hundred feet apart.[20] Also in 1913, the Village of Waterloo designated street numbers for houses and businesses so that free postal delivery could be instituted on September 1, 1913.[21] The Waterloo village board on May 6, 1914, resolved to have East Main, Washington and River Streets paved as part of the new state highway law, by which the state, the county, the village and adjoining property owners would pay for the improvement.[22]

The rapid increase in the number of automobiles led to the development of many auto-related businesses, such as gas stations and tourist cabins. One of the most interesting examples in Seneca County was the Windmill Tourist Camp just west of Seneca Falls. The windmill itself was built in 1929. The camp had a total of fifteen cabins, as many as nine gas pumps, a restaurant and a gift shop. It should be noted that the rise of the automobile helps to explain the demise of streetcars and railroads in the county and nationwide.[23]

In 2007, there were 28,143 registered automobiles in Seneca County for a population of about 33,000 and a total of 24,758 driver's licenses.[24] In 2013, there were 28,910 vehicle registrations and 23,738 driver's licenses.[25]

When people see a really old car, such as a Tin Lizzie, while they are driving on a highway it prompts strong reactions, and for good reasons. In part, it's simply because cars today look so different than those early cars. And perhaps those old cars allow us to think nostalgically of a time when the pace of living—and life itself—was so different.

5

Uncovering the History of the Backbone Ridge

The Backbone Ridge is the name given to the hilltop ridge that runs between Seneca and Cayuga Lakes and today is the center of the Finger Lakes National Forest. Its history is a microcosm of the larger economic, social and political transformations that have taken place in American society since 1900.[26]

Following the Revolutionary War, white settlers moved into this area, part of the Military Tract, as farmers. These early settlers cleared the land for the production of hay and small grains, such as buckwheat. As New York City grew, a strong market for these products developed, encouraging more intensive agriculture. The farmers prospered until about 1900. By that time, soil depletion

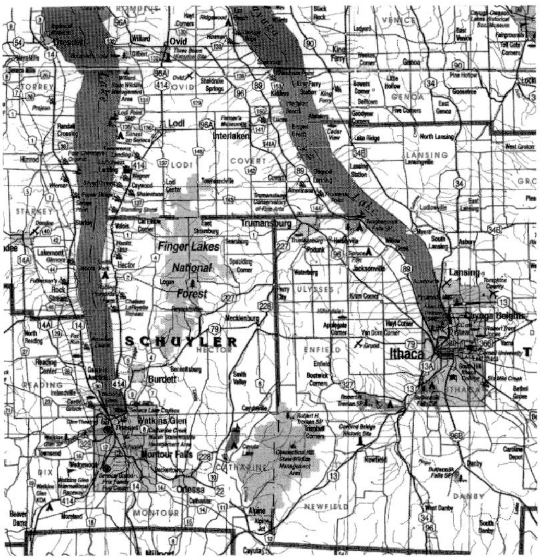

The Backbone Ridge refers to the high-elevation area between Cayuga and Seneca Lakes, with portions in southern Seneca County and northern Schuyler and Tompkins Counties. *Seneca County Historian's Office.*

and increasing competition from the Midwest made farming in the Hector Hills area less feasible. Between 1890 and the Great Depression, over one million acres of farmland were abandoned in south central New York State. In the 1930s, it was recognized that farmers in many parts of the country could no longer make a living from their exhausted land. Environmental damage was occurring as land was cultivated more and more intensively to make ends meet.

During the Great Depression, the U.S. government, through its Resettlement Administration, stepped in to buy many farms and help relocate their residents to better land or other jobs. With the passage of the Bankhead-Jones Act in 1937, the Farm Security Administration acquired over one hundred farms in the Backbone Ridge between 1938 and 1941.[27] Because the purchase of farms was done on a willing-seller, willing-buyer basis, the resulting federal ownership resembled a patchwork quilt. This was especially true in Seneca County. There, the soils were more productive, and some of the families elected to stay on their farms rather than sell to the federal government. The newly acquired federal land, named the Hector Land Use Area (LUA), was initially managed by the Soil Conservation Service. The emphasis was on the stabilization of the soil by planting

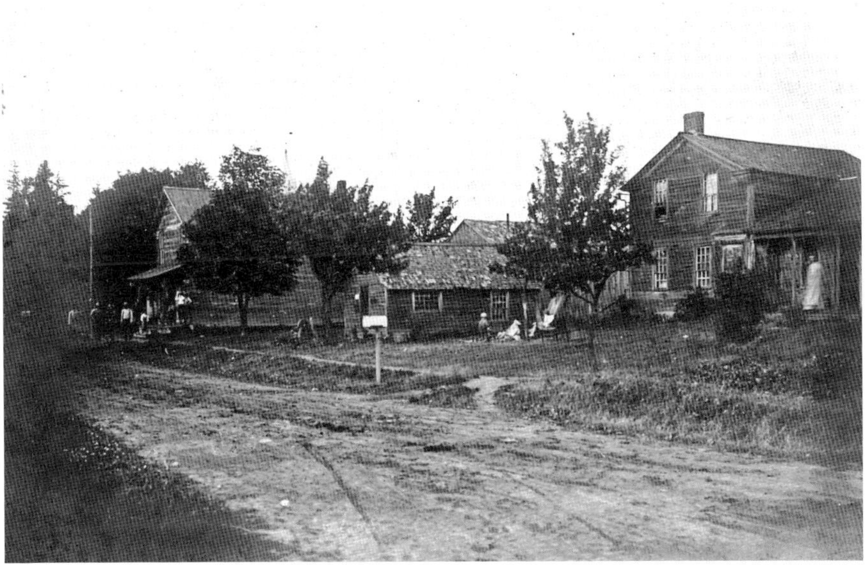

A common perception in the late 1930s was that Backbone Ridge farms were marginal and the federal government should buy them so the owners could start over in a better economic setting. *Backbone Ridge History Group.*

conifers and the development of a grazing program. Previously cultivated fields were converted to improved pastures to demonstrate how less-intensive agriculture could still make productive use of the land.

The Hector Cooperative Grazing Association was informally started in 1938 and formally incorporated in April 1946. This organization was issued a long-term lease to manage grazing on the Hector LUA. This organization coordinated use of the pastures by as many as 120 individual livestock owners within a one-hundred-mile radius. Farmers who paid dues to the association would bring their animals in the spring to graze on the land; the animals were then rounded up in the fall. From 1939 to 1971, the association made use of other resources of the land by harvesting timber, cutting and selling posts, leasing hay lots and cutting and selling Christmas trees and firewood. In 1941, sheep were the primary livestock grazed, but there were also both beef and dairy cattle, as well as small herds of horses. There were initially 138 members of the association, but that number dropped to 64 in 1992 and 35 in 2012. In 2012, the association used 4,500 acres for grazing in thirty-five pastures with eighty miles of fence.[28]

By the 1950s, many of the original objectives of the Hector Land Use Area had been met. Farmers had been resettled, the eroding soil stabilized and alternative agriculture uses demonstrated. At the same time, the public was becoming interested in the concept of multiple uses of public land. Management and private ownership of the Hector LUA was reevaluated. In 1954, the decision was made to transfer administrative responsibilities to the U.S. Forest Service.[29]

In the 1970s, the Hector LUA was identified as some of the possible lands to resolve the Cayuga Indian Land Claim. The discussion centered on a total of 3,629 acres in Seneca County, comprising 27 percent of the total land base of the county.[30] This out-of-court settlement did not materialize, and the Cayugas filed a formal court case in 1980.

In 1982, the Hector area was identified by the federal government as one of the federal land use areas that would be considered excess to Forest Service needs and could thus be sold under existing authority without review by Congress. This touched off a massive local protest effort. A total of 520 comments from the public were received, along with seven petitions with more than 8,200 signatures of those opposing the sale. Because of strong opposition to the proposal, Congressmen Frank Horton and Stan Lundine introduced legislation to officially incorporate the Hector area into the Green Mountain Forest system so that it could not be sold without approval by Congress.

National forest status was given to the former Hector LUA lands by Congress on November 29, 1983. At that time, the forest consisted of a checkerboard pattern of parcels totaling about 13,000 acres.[31] In October 1985, the area was renamed the Hector Ranger District, Finger Lakes National Forest. Today, the Finger Lakes National Forest, which consists of 16,212 acres, is still an administrative unit of the Green Mountain National Forest. Although about 3.2 million acres of New York State is in the state forest preserves, wildlife management areas and forests, the Finger Lakes National Forest is the only national forest in all of New York State![32]

The Finger Lakes National Forest (FLNF) today is composed of these farmlands and remnants of the past, such as old stone walls, cellar holes, stone foundations, wells and cemeteries that dot the landscape. Dr. Lou Ann Wurst (formerly of SUNY College at Brockport) has been leading archaeology students for the past several summers in excavations at farms located at the south end of the forest.[33] The goal of the project is to understand the everyday lives of farm families from initial settlement in the early 1800s until the farms were finally abandoned. Their preliminary work suggests that farm families on the Backbone Ridge were making capital investments to improve their farms, changing their agricultural production strategies to match current markets and investing in costly consumer goods such as automobiles, telephones, radios and domestic objects well into the twentieth century. These results contradict the commonly held belief that farming in this part of the country declined over a long period of time and indicate that the history of agriculture in this area is much more complex than is typically assumed.[34]

Realizing that the history of this area prior to the Great Depression might be forgotten and even lost with the death of so many of the era's residents, the Backbone Ridge History Group (BRHG) was formed in 2006. The BRHG is a grass-roots organization that

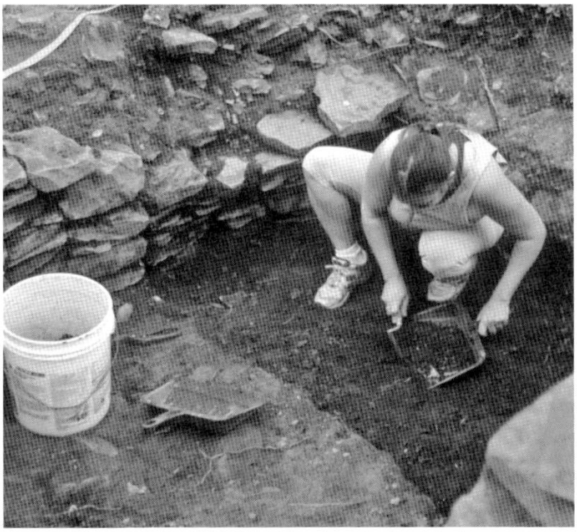

Several summer archaeological studies have been conducted on the Backbone Ridge. *Backbone Ridge History Group.*

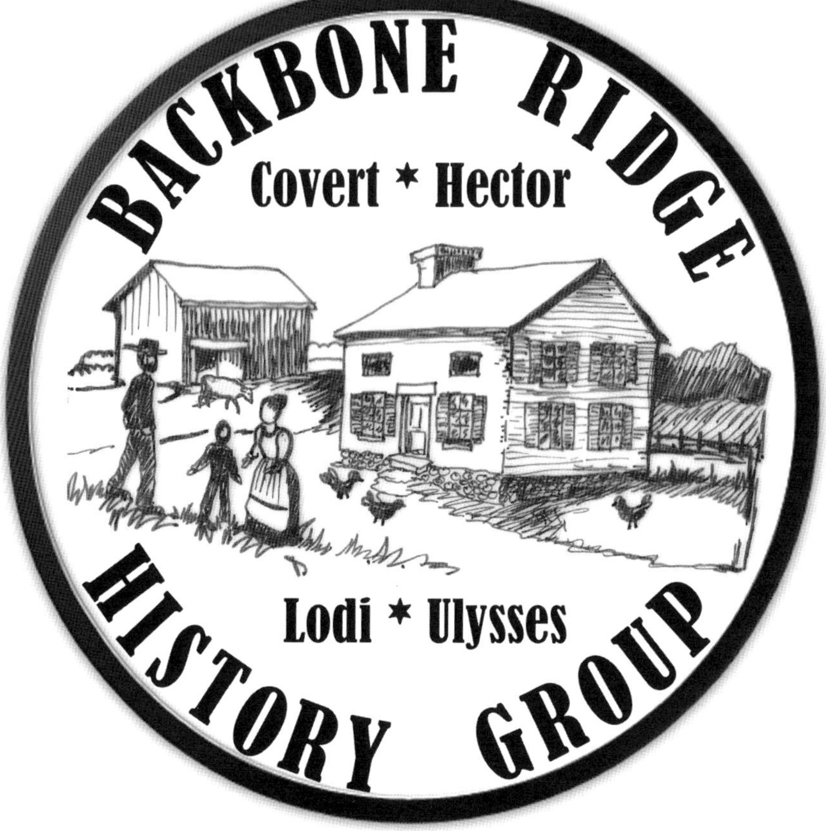

Since its establishment in 2006, the Backbone Ridge History Group has done much to promote awareness of the history of the Backbone Ridge area. *Backbone Ridge History Group.*

collects the history of the land and the people in the Backbone Ridge area. The group is very interested in this area, because the Backbone Ridge was once heavily populated with people, farms and towns. It was dramatically changed through purchases by the Resettlement Administration.[35] The BRHG has adopted the following mission statement:

> *To identify, collect, interpret and in cooperation with surrounding historical societies, to facilitate access to archives and artifacts related to the history of the lands, communities and people on and around the Backbone Ridge and to share this history with others.*[36]

Given the aging of the population that has lived in this area prior to the purchases by the Resettlement Administration, the Backbone Ridge History Group is initially focusing its energies on identifying existing primary-source information about the area and encouraging the preservation of these irreplaceable documents and artifacts. The BRHG secured three Documentary Heritage Project Grants from the New York State Archives to help with these efforts.

The Backbone Ridge History Group was the recipient on October 26, 2009, of the Debra E. Bernhardt Annual Archives Award for Excellence in Documenting New York's History. Quoting from the award notification letter:

> *This award is presented by the Board of Regents and the State Archives to an organization in New York State that has demonstrated leadership in improving the documentary record of New York State....This year's award recognizes the Backbone Ridge History Group for its efforts in facilitating partnerships between organizations and individuals in Seneca and Schuyler counties interested in the history of lands now part of the Finger Lakes National Forest and promoting the study of that history in the Documenting Land Use and Population on the Hector Backbone project. The BRHG is commended for taking on collaboration among so many small organizations. The group is visionary in its simultaneous emphasis on both the documentation and use of records, and admirable in the dedication and skills of its team.*

The Backbone Ridge History Group continues its mission through research, oral history interviews, collection of historic documents, cemetery cleanup and restoration, publications, a website, public educational programs and exhibits throughout the area.

6

A History of Cayuga Lake Park

Earliest History of the Park

Long before Cayuga Lake State Park was established in 1928, area residents were frequenting at least two "private parks" in the general area of Bridgeport and south to where the state park is located today. These two private parks were Bull's Grove and Wayne's Grove. The latter was located on part of what is today the lake portion of Cayuga Lake State Park. Bull's Grove was located farther north. The popularity of these private parks in an era before central air conditioning is no surprise. People would spend a hot Sunday at the lake, swimming or simply catching a cool breeze off the lake.

In 1886, a group of New York City businessmen purchased Wayne's Woods. The company, the Cayuga Lake Park Company, had as its incorporators George H. Staynor, John D. Haines and William J. Townsend. Its trustees were Staynor, C.D. Haines, A.G. Haines, D.S. Haines and J.D. Haines. The company had a capital stock of $20,000, divided into two hundred shares. The articles of incorporation stated that the company's objectives were to erect a suitable park building or buildings for holding fairs, meetings, exhibitions and other entertainments—"terms which describe in a general way the improvements contemplated at the grove."[37] The property, purchased by the company from William G. Wayne for $10,000, included Wayne's Grove, with its lakefront and enough land in the rear to encompass fifty acres in all.[38]

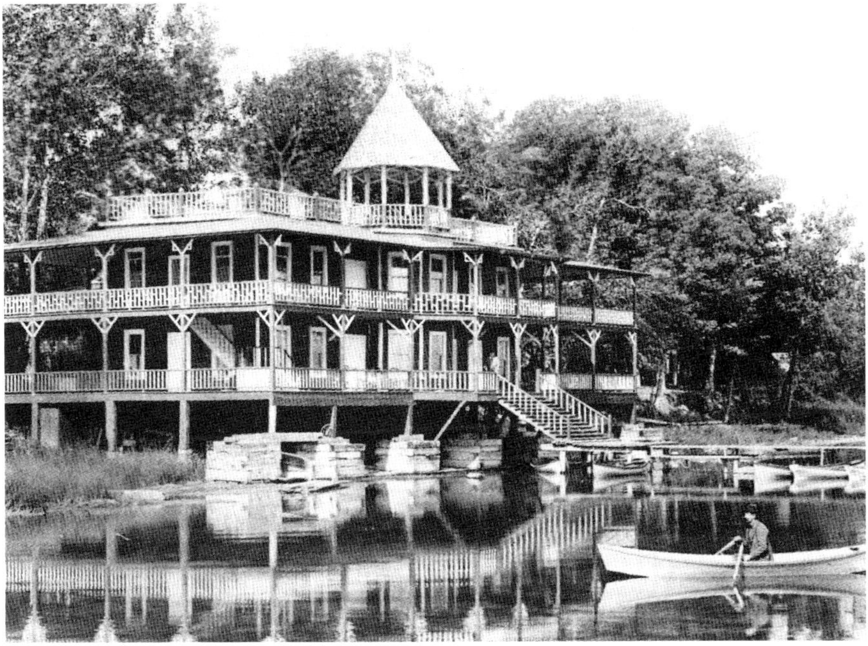

Bull's Grove, along with Wayne's Grove, was a private amusement park located in the area where Cayuga Lake Park was later established. *Seneca County Historian's Office.*

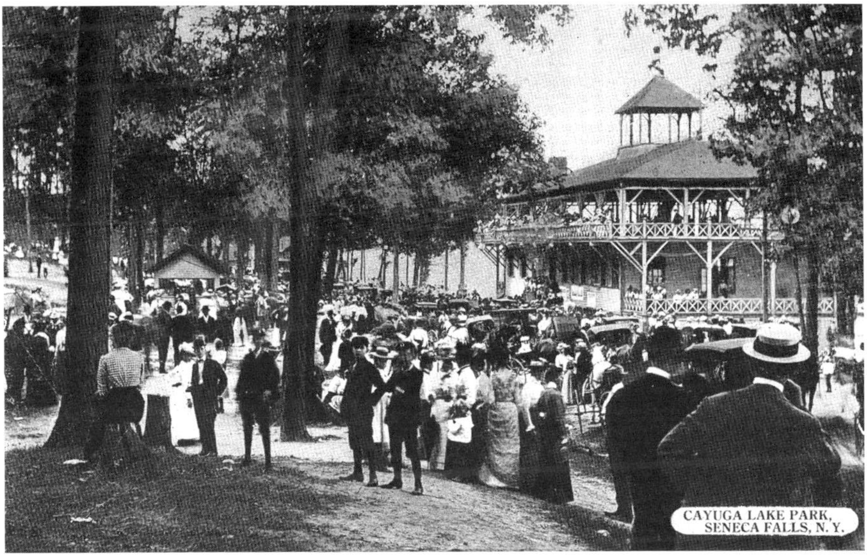

Cayuga Lake Park was very popular, especially on the weekends, from the 1890s until about 1920. *Seneca County Historian's Office.*

Prior to this purchase, another company, the Seneca Falls, Restvale and Cayuga Lake Street Railroad, had been established to build a street railroad from the Village of Seneca Falls to Cayuga Lake. The firm's incorporators were DeWitt C. Hadcock, J. Marshall Guion, Weed Barnum, Nelson Duntz, Peter Troutman, William B. Rubert, S.B. Johnson, Fred Maier, William E. Rubert, Frank Westcott, John McKeon, Thomas Farron and David Cushman. It is significant that the incorporators of this company, unlike those of the Cayuga Lake Park Company, were all local citizens. Its capital stock was $30,000. The company officers were DeWitt C. Hadcock (president), David Cushman (vice president) and Peter Troutman (secretary and treasurer). After a few months surveying possible routes, the company chose one starting at the corner of Bridge and Bayard Streets and proceeding east to Restvale Cemetery, then south to the village limits and east through Wayne's Road to the lake.[39] This meant that the new railroad line would basically be an extension of the existing Seneca Falls and Waterloo Railroad's line to the lake, from the Franklin House on Bridge Street in Seneca Falls to the new Cayuga Lake Park.[40]

The existing Seneca Falls and Waterloo Railroad, however, did not want this competing railroad company to succeed. It had been contemplating

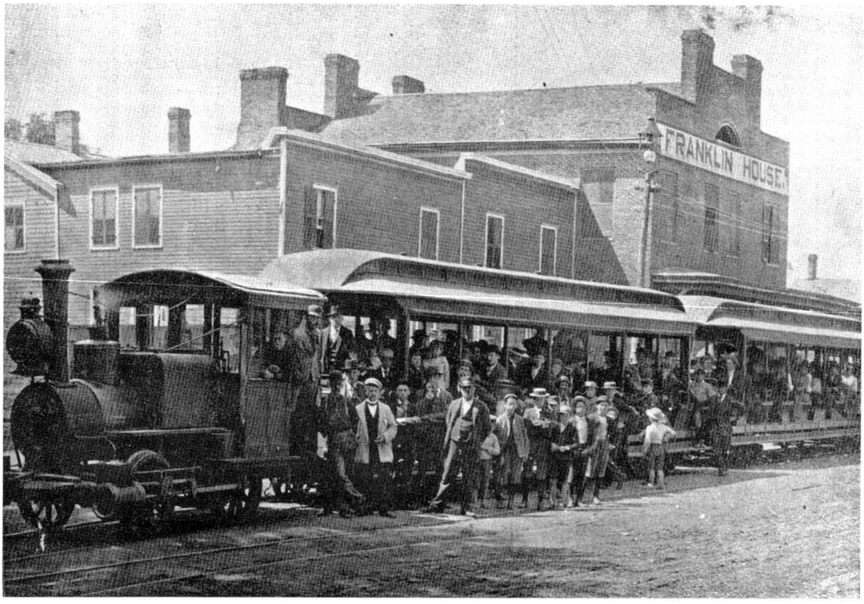

Seneca Falls residents could board the trolley at the Franklin House to ride to Cayuga Lake Park. *Philomena Cammuso.*

building its own line to Cayuga Lake and quickly began construction of a rail line on Bayard Street.

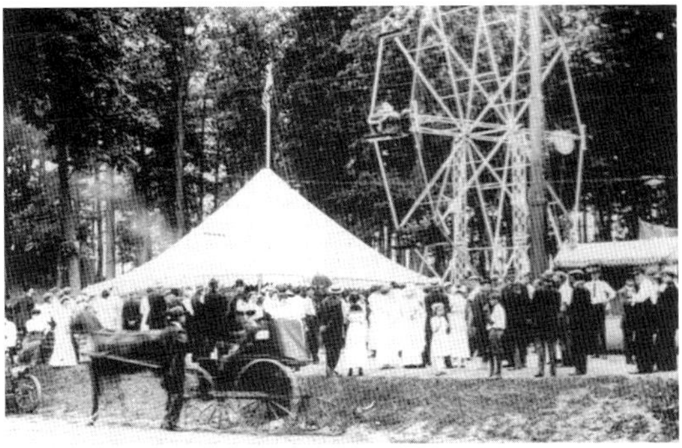

The Ferris wheel was one of the most popular rides at Cayuga Lake Park. *Seneca County Historian's Office.*

Although the village mayor tried to stop the Seneca Falls and Waterloo Railroad Company, that firm apparently "won out" because of its cooperation with the Cayuga Lake Park Company. The latter company changed its original plans so that the railroad line terminus would be at Bull's Grove instead of at Wayne's Grove. A summer hotel would be built at Wayne's Grove.[41] The dispute was resolved, and the railroad was formally opened on August 19, 1886. This was the first standard-gauge railroad line ever built in the country for the primary purpose of reaching a summer resort.[42] The first railroad was steam-powered. It was soon replaced by an electric line. The train service then consisted of three passenger coaches and made the trip every half hour throughout the afternoon and evening.

Facilities at the park were expanded because of the large numbers of people who came, especially on Sundays. Among the amenities were baseball fields. The wires of the Thomson-Houston Electric Company were extended to the park, illuminating the resort and providing a grand sight, especially from the lake. A new opera house capable of holding five hundred people was built. It often hosted stage acts by New York City performers. There were fireworks at the pier. By June 1887, a steamboat was making regular trips on Cayuga Lake to the park's pier.[43]

On July 4, 1887, it was estimated that twenty-five thousand people were present for the celebration of the nation's birthday, described as follows by the *Seneca Falls Reveille*:

> *At prompt 12:00 midnight, the fun commenced, and continued to 12:00 last night. Cannons and cannon firecrackers roared, fourth of July bonfires were fired, and until daybreak young America successfully sought against the attempts of Old Morpheus to entrap his victims in slumber. At daybreak, the Independent Battery of Geneva opened its festivities*

> *by a salute of 38 guns, and the church bells, shop bells and whistles joined in. The pioneer parade in the morning was a unique representation of the times of Job Smith, the first settler.... The industrial parade at 1:00 in the afternoon was a well-represented exhibition of the village industries.... The military and firemens' parade took place at 3:00.... After the military and firemens parade, the literary exercises took place at the Opera house.... The fireworks display in the evening was one of the grandest ever made in western New York.*[44]

In 1887, many changes were made to Cayuga Lake Park. The lakeside pavilion was modified to provide facilities for women and children. The opera house was converted into a dance hall and skating rink. A steam yacht, connecting with New York City passenger trains, could now bring tourists from the Cayuga, New York station to this park. A balloon ascension attracted visitors, as did ballgames, church picnics and rowing races. There was also a professional regatta.[45]

No liquor was sold at the park, and gambling was not allowed. A weekly column in the *Reveille* reported events at the park. A camp meeting for African Americans, with jubilee singers, was held. Church groups came from Auburn and Clyde, and there was a reunion picnic for Odd Fellows lodges between Syracuse and Rochester. The railroad line reported that it sold 1,574 tickets on one Saturday when there was a ballgame. At the end of August 1887, it was reported that four thousand persons were present at the park one Saturday.[46]

In an article for the *Reveille* on July 14, 1965, Elizabeth Delavan remembered these early trolley-car days of Cayuga Lake Park:

> *Back in the trolley-car era, the Park was gay, high-keyed, a little fresh, whereas today's State Park has taken on the dignity of those fine oak trees, now grown so tall and protecting....*
>
> *A ride from Seneca Falls to the Park in the day of the Trolley Car was inexpensive, pleasantly scenic and of short duration. The trip ended in Wayne's Grove, at the foot of a slope, where the lake lay spread out and sparkling a few hundred feet ahead. From this terminus the visitor walked through aisles of green park benches in the direction of his particular interest—for the Park had several distinct activity areas, each attractive in its own way.*
>
> *The most wholesome and certainly at times the most satisfying was Wayne's, that magic name associated with the best ice cream ever made, and lemonade of excellence. You could buy other things there too....*

From the restaurant which was near the north end of the Park, a stroll along the cinder path bordering the dusty road brought one to the dance pavilion, a two-story square summery structure framed in offices. A wide pier stretched before it far out into the water to greet the incoming steamers and little boats looking for a tie-up.

Across the road from the dance pavilion, near the center of the Park, was a sort of miniature midway offering a merry-go-round, sometimes a Ferris wheel, and one season a lovely brown bear in a pen. There were other attractions, they varied from year to year.

The Park ended on the south at a high wooden fence a little beyond the merry-go-round. Just about where the present horseshoe pitching court is located, there used to be some unimposing buildings referred to collectively as The Saloons; but that was beyond the fence, and definitely out of bounds.

A visit to the Park was high adventure for one of impressionable age. Every merry-go-round ride held the thrill of the brass ring you snatched as your horse pranced by…entitling you to a free ride.

The dance floor was romantic…when viewed through the windows of the veranda—although dancing there was forbidden to some growing up in the era when exacting parents believed that dancing should be supervised….

Besides Sunday School picnics there were other picnics of assorted sizes and origins spread under the park trees, among the mosquitoes, on those long, hot summer days. The baskets and blankets and watermelons as well as the passengers all rode down together to the Park on the Trolley….

The early Park was used by local people; there it was—there was the trolley to take them to it—the trolley went nowhere else….The early Park catered to merry makers. Today's facility encourages purposeful activities—camping, hiking, swimming. In the Trolley Car days the electric lights of concessions and the pavilion used to light up a gay and garish setting of commercialism; today, wood fires flicker serenely these summer evenings before the trailer and cabins, or around the picnic tables.[47]

Many park visitors came by steamboat until 1907. The steamboats *Frontenac* and *Mohawk* regularly traveled Cayuga Lake daily on round trips, making stops at the dock at Cayuga Lake Park. This commercial steamboat travel dropped off after the *Frontenac* caught fire and sank on July 27, 1907, with the death of eight passengers. More people owned their own personal motorboats and automobiles.[48]

A popular amusement at Cayuga Lake Park for many years was the "toboggon ride." "Both young and old alike rode on the toboggon which shot over the

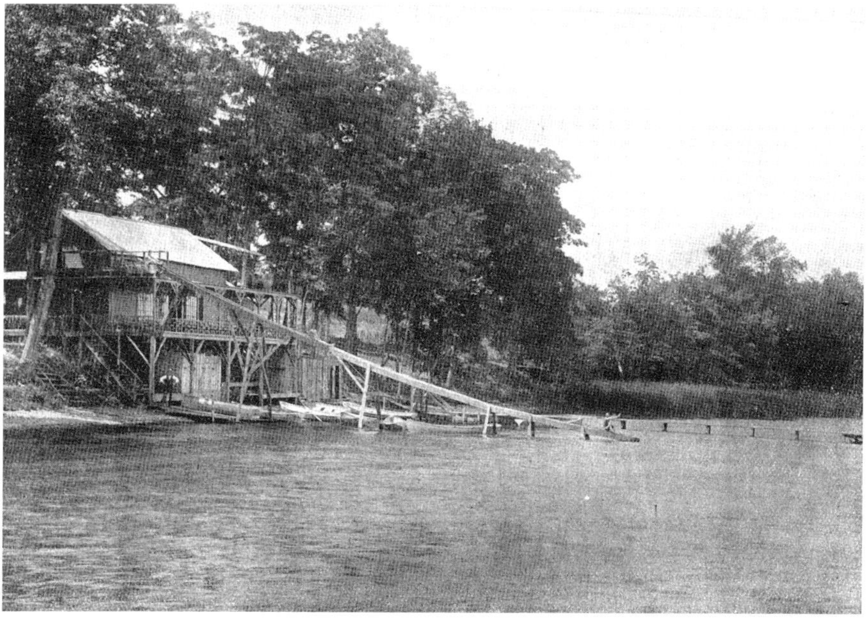

A popular ride at Cayuga Lake Park was the "toboggan slide," which plunged riders into the lake. *Philomena Cammuso.*

wooden rollers of the chute with a terrific roar and carried the thrill seeker out into the lake." In 1915, this toboggon ride was replaced with "The Shoots."

STEPS LEADING TO THE ESTABLISHMENT OF CAYUGA LAKE STATE PARK

The advent of the automobile reduced ridership on the trolley line to Cayuga Lake Park. As early as 1914, the Geneva, Seneca Falls and Auburn Railroad Company, which at that time owned the park and the trolley line to the park, threatened to close the park.[49] In June 1921, the railroad company formally petitioned the New York State Public Service Commission for permission to abandon the line. In September 1921, the railroad company voted at its annual meeting to abandon its line east from Seneca Falls to Cayuga Lake Park as unprofitable.[50]

With the demise of the trolley in 1921, Matthew Hamill of Seneca Falls purchased the fifty acres of Cayuga Lake Park, including the grove and pavilion, in order to improve and lease it. By May 1922, the park had been cleaned up for the first time in several years. The dirt road through the park was in good condition. A new bathhouse, slides and chutes were soon to be put into operation.[51]

By the end of 1923, there were expectations that Cayuga Lake Park might be incorporated into the State Park Plan, authorized by the state legislature in 1922. It was not, however, included in the initial parks established in the Finger Lakes. In September 1927, the Seneca Falls Business Association presented a detailed proposal to the Finger Lakes Park Commission for the creation of Red Jacket State Park at the site. The two key individuals in this proposal were A.S. Hughes and Murray Hilbert. The Finger Lakes Park Commission voted to support creation of a state park at this site, but keeping the old title of Cayuga Lake Park. On October 15, 1927, the State Council on Parks gave its approval to the state to acquire the park, and Governor Alfred E. Smith gave his approval on October 25. Cyrus Garnsey Jr. offered additional lake frontage from his farm for park purposes. In 1928, a total of 125.98 acres were acquired for Cayuga Lake State Park. In that year, three new Finger Lakes parks were named as state parks: Fair Haven, Stony Brook and Cayuga Lake State Park.[52]

EARLY YEARS AS CAYUGA LAKE STATE PARK

Soon after its becoming a state park, much development work took place at the site. This work included the construction of a dock, parking area, camp and picnic and bathing facilities. Beach improvement and building repairs were also undertaken. The park's appearance had been greatly improved. The old brick powerhouse and small stand near the pavilion had been removed; benches were repaired and repainted; and new rustic picnic tables were made. In addition, eighteen hundred feet of water pipe were laid.[53]

The first outing at Cayuga Lake State Park was in July 1928 by the Married People's Club of the First Presbyterian Church. They used the pavilion, which had been thoroughly restored with lighting, plumbing and other service equipment.[54]

Governor Franklin D. Roosevelt visited the park on Friday, July 18, 1930, as part of his tour of the Barge Canal system. He spoke to an audience of about 2,000 people, preceded by a dinner party for about 250 in the pavilion. His speech lasted over an hour. Throngs of people filled the pavilion's dance floor and porches. Police officers sought to keep the attending crowd back from the pavilion veranda, fearing the structure might collapse.[55]

In 1928, Cayuga Lake Park camping fee receipts were $147, second only to Taughannock.

More development and improvements came in the next few years. In 1929, $40,000 was expended to enlarge the Cayuga Lake State Park beach area and to dredge for a boat harbor. On August 24, 1932, a new pavilion was dedicated. It had been built at a cost of $35,000 and was erected on the site of the former larger pavilion. Dancing continued at this new pavilion. A new automatic player piano was installed in 1933. In 1932, the parking area was enlarged and a new heating system in the pavilion was installed. This made the pavilion available for winter sports. Because of the economic hardships stemming from the Depression, the state appropriated $22,500 in TERA (Temporary Emergence Relief Administration) funds to improve Cayuga Lake State Park. These funds were used to erect a new storage building and paint shop, grading and graveling of the parking area, placing 2,500 pounds of sand on the bathing beach, topsoil and planting installed on the beach front, graveling of the park road connecting Route 89 and the camping area, grading and graveling of one thousand feet of trail, the construction of stone steps and flagstone walks near the pavilion and extension of the water supply system. In 1933, additional TERA-funded work was done to improve the park.

In 1935, Cayuga Lake Park became part of a Civilian Conservation Corps (CCC) project funded by the federal government. Construction of thirteen buildings making up the CCC camp was completed at the end of July. As many as two hundred young men, largely from the Hudson River Valley and New York City areas, worked on various projects and were "inculcated [with the] American ideas of life, thought, and work, in addition to instilling wholesome respect for authority, work and education."[56] In 1936, the CCC youth constructed a shelter pavilion in the picnic grove; six cabins; a two-acre trailer and tent-site area; and more picnic tables, benches and fireplaces. They also created additional parking and trail facilities and hauled in two thousand yards of sand to improve the bathing beach. In 1937, the CCC youth graded and planted the side slopes of the state highway through the park, installed concrete curbs along the lake road, added sand to the beach and graded several trails and parking areas. The CCC program at this park was ended in July 1937.[57]

BITS AND PIECES OF MORE RECENT HISTORY

George A. Dobson retired in December 1938 as the superintendent of Cayuga Lake State Park. He had begun working at the state park as a caretaker in June 1928, shortly after the site became a state park.[58]

In the fall of 1942, two recreation buildings at the park were used as housing for construction workers at the Seneca Ordnance Depot and Sampson Naval Training Center, stemming from the serious local housing shortage.

Interestingly, in 1952, the state condemned the swimming facilities as off-limits to airmen from Sampson Air Force Base; pollution from raw sewage was flowing into Cayuga's waters. (The military standards were higher than those for civilian use.)[59]

During the summer of 1954, the director of the Seneca County Health Department said the diving-area water was dangerously polluted by human waste from nearby cottages. The beach was closed to swimmers in August.

In August 1958, park superintendent James Henry told the Seneca Falls Kiwanians that Cayuga Lake State Park was the most popular park in the state. At that point in 1958, he said, a total of 102,697 people had attended the park. The picnic area could accommodate 5,000. About 35 campers were turned away each day. There were forty-seven tent sites, nineteen trailer sites and fourteen cabins. The west side of the camping area was being developed to create three hundred more tent/trailer sites and three shower buildings.[60]

The pollution problems in Cayuga Lake continued to demand attention. In 1977, a research and field survey team from Eisenhower College conducted a survey of areas to be impacted by the proposed extension of the Village of Seneca Falls sewer system to the town. This sewer system was finally initiated in 1981.[61]

In 1976, a total of 136,000 people attended the park. A 1978 survey showed that 94.4 percent of park visitors arrived by automobile and that 80.6 percent came from the Finger Lakes area.[62]

In 2007–8, park attendance was 166,766, an increase of about 25,000 from the previous two years.[63]

CONCLUDING REMARKS

In the early 1930s, C.R. Rosenberry wrote a piece titled "Rambling Round Cayuga State Park." What follows is a portion of what he had to say about the park:

> *An earlier generation in Seneca Falls and its neighbor towns used to pack its lunch, pile into trolley cars, and enjoy happy days at Cayuga Lake Park.*
>
> *There it rode the merry-go-round and the "ocean wave," bathed in the lake at a time when bathing suits were tenfold more ample than today, listened to band concerts and vaudeville, and watched the first flickering attempts at moving pictures.*
>
> *In the heyday of Cayuga Lake Park, the three floors of the big pavilion were often packed with gaily-bedecked merry makers, and sometimes there weren't street cars enough to get them all home until after midnight, which was very late, in the Nineties.*
>
> *The local street railway company had built the pavilion and developed the amusement park as a magnet for fares, and it was a good investment—until the automobile age put a crimp in it!*
>
> *After a while the trolley line was abandoned and weeds began to grow in the grove where joyous picnickers had one time roamed. The pavilion was still used for dances, but that was about all, and the property came to be owned by a man named Matthew Hamill. From him the State purchased it to revive its popularity as a park—but a very different kind of park.*
>
> *Cayuga Lake State Park has a long frontage on the lake only two miles from its outlet. Old Cayuga, with her reputation for danger, for stern depths and chill waters, is in a kindlier mood at her northern extremity. Shallow—a tall man could almost wade across at the point—the water is perpetually warm for the swimmers.*
>
> *This park, too, has its distinct individuality. Aside from the lake view and the tall grove of oaks on the rolling hillside, it has no special scenic values to offer. Its tone is more one of pleasantness and holiday relaxation. Here you can go to rest, rather than to ramble through long gorges and listen to roaring waterfalls* [as in other nearby parks].
>
> *Cayuga Lake Park has one of the two real sand beaches in the Finger Lakes, and a beautiful pavilion and bath house, built in Swiss Chalet style, facing the waterfront. A thousand feet long, the beach is amply wide to permit thousands of people to enjoy sun-bathing, and it extends far enough out under water to provide a soft cushion for the toes of those who prefer water-bathing.*

> *Cayuga Lake is a gem in that necklace of parks and scenic beauty spots along the Cayuga Lake Boulevard extending northward from Ithaca to Lake Ontario. This new road passes through the center of this park and will doubtless bring far greater visitation than it now enjoys.*
>
> *One of the joys of the park is its large picnic and camping grove, whose carpet is mainly greensward but underneath which much of the characteristic Finger Lakes planting has been done—flowering shrubs, azalea, mountain laurel, rhododendron, and the like.*
>
> *The park area extends back up the gentle hillside from the lakeshore for some distance, covering 250 acres or more. The grove will sometime be extended. Above that is an athletic field with a baseball diamond fit for the "Big Leagues" to use.*
>
> *Historically, Cayuga Lake State Park points with pride to the association of the celebrated Seneca Indian Chief, Red Jacket, within its neighborhood. This most renowned of Indian orators was born nearby and a monument has been erected in his honor.*
>
> *A spacious boat harbor at the southern end of the park is one of the improvements. Here all sizes of boats, from motor launches to rowboats, find haven.*
>
> *The park is sandwiched between popular cottage areas, the lakeshore for many miles being dotted with attractive summer dwellings.*[64]

The New York State Parks website describes the park's terrain as "flat at lakeshore, where the beach and sun lawns are, then slopes gently uphill to campsites and cabins. The scenic highlight of the park is the expansive view of Cayuga Lake. In the shallow water near the park, largemouth bass, bullheads and carp thrive. In deeper water, anglers can catch northern pike, smallmouth bass, lake trout, landlocked salmon and many other varieties of fish. The park has a boat launch, playground, playing field."[65] Another website states that there are currently 267 campsites, fourteen cabins and one full-service cottage.[66] People come from all over to camp there.

7
Cobblestone Buildings

Part A: The Nature of Cobblestone Buildings

As Rich and Sue Freeman say so well in the introduction to their 2005 book *Cobblestone Quest*, upstate New York residents drive by cobblestone houses and usually give them very little thought. Most people barely recognize that this area was the pre–Civil War birthplace of a new form of construction. It's a method that remains peculiar to our region; over 90 percent of the cobblestone buildings in the entire United States are located within a sixty-five-mile radius of Rochester. Estimates vary, but approximately seven hundred to twelve hundred cobblestone buildings were erected in the United States. Between six hundred and nine hundred of them are in New York State, spread over twenty-five counties, from the Hudson River to Niagara Falls.[67]

Using an Ice Age residue of glacially rounded native stones, pioneer craftsmen in the middle third of the nineteenth century perfected a form of folk art that was without precedent in America.[68] The cobblestone craft that developed in the Greater Rochester area flourished, spread and died out within less than half a century. Nevertheless, it left its stamp on the region. According to Rich and Sue Freeman, it holds a place in history as the last generation of completely hand-built houses.[69]

While this chapter deals with cobblestone buildings as a construction method, not an architectural style, it can be said that most cobblestone buildings are Greek Revival in style. Those constructed before 1835 were, however, usually in the Federal style. There are rare instances of cobblestone buildings in the Gothic Revival and/or Italianate style.[70] With few exceptions, the cobblestone era ended with the beginning of the Civil War. There are three time periods of cobblestone architecture: the early period (1825–35), the middle period (1835–45) and the late period (1845–61).[71] During the early period, masons predominantly used glacial field cobbles and built with crude, irregular designs.[72] Stones used in early cobblestone construction varied considerably in size and were laid in uneven rows. One of the first stylistic innovations was to lay stones in more even rows. During this period, stones were from two and a half to three and a half inches high and from three to six inches long. Stones were sized by passing them through holes cut in a board or through iron rings called "beetle rings."[73] Early cobblestone buildings were typically constructed with an eighteen- to twenty-inch-thick, solid coursed rubble wall with three rows of field cobbles tied together with elongated or triangular stones. The inner two-thirds of the wall used large stones. There was complete integration of the cobblestone surface with the interior wall—the whole wall was laid up as one. To finish off the interior wall, a horsehair plaster was applied to the stone.[74]

In the middle period, smaller stones that were rounded or oval water-washed stones were commonly used. Sometimes, water-washed stones were mixed in with glacial fieldstones.[75] The size of the cobblestones used was from one and a half to two and a half inches high and from two to four inches long. Masons began to use stones of one particular color, with red sandstones being especially popular.[76] These masons also became quite competitive for originality in their designs.[77] The typical middle period cobblestone building was constructed with a rubble core. A facing of cobblestones was laid on front of the core, with longer cobbles extending into the building. The entire wall was laid up as one.[78]

During the late period, the cobblestone buildings were typically constructed with uniform small, round, single-color stones, especially on the "front" (street) side.[79] "Small" meant one to one and a half inches high and three-quarters of an inch to two inches wide. A herringbone pattern was often used, as was a design of alternate rows of white and red stones.[80] In many cases, the cobbles served as a "veneer" against a structural rubble stone wall. The construction was often criticized for being monotonous and machine-made in appearance. Critics felt that "craftsmanship" had given way to "skill."[81] Some of the late period cobblestone buildings were constructed with a rubble wall laid first; a mortar and small-stone veneer was laid separately. In this process, there was no bonding between the two, making this the least-permanent construction design of the cobblestone building techniques. Typically, wall thickness would vary, with twenty-inch-thick cellar and first-floor walls and eighteen-inch second-floor walls. In some cases, sixteen-inch-thick walls were used throughout. Furring strips would be applied to the interior walls to provide an air space (sometimes two to three inches thick) between the stone and the interior wall. The interior wall would then be finished by lath and plaster.[82]

The demise of cobblestone construction coincided with the outbreak of the Civil War. There are several reasons for this. One obvious factor is that the war caused inflation, making masonry labor simply too expensive. A second factor is that the local supply of small stones became more difficult to come by, leading to rising costs of transporting the stones from farther away. Finally, cobblestone construction was replaced by more efficient technologies, such as the wooden balloon frame, fast-drying Portland cement and mass-produced bricks.[83]

The term *cobblestone* needs explanation. Geologists classify stones by size: "pebble," "cobblestone" or "boulder." In lay terms, a pebble is a stone held by two fingers; a cobblestone is a stone held by one hand; and a boulder needs two hands to hold it. So, "cobblestones" can be between 2.5 and 10.1 inches (or 64 to 256 millimeters) in size. The word *cobblestone* comes from Middle English: "cob" means a rounded lump; "ston" means a small rock.[84]

The cobblestones of our area were laid down as glacial deposits from the Ice Age about one million years ago. The ice and water polished the rocks and scattered them throughout the topsoil and subsoil of the lands, even miles away from Lake Ontario.[85] Cobblestones in our area can be differentiated as either "fieldstones" or "water-rounded stones," depending on where human beings have picked them up out of the ground and their physical appearance. Fieldstones are angular stones gathered from glacial till and outwash deposits from the glaciers. Water-rounded stones are also glacially derived but have been rounded by wave action, either along the Lake Ontario shore or, long ago, by a glacial lake and then left in an outwashed deposit.[86] These stones were plentiful and had to be removed from the soil so that the land could be farmed. Using the picked-up stones as building material was a fortunate result.

Cobblestone construction did not originate in New York. As far back as the third century AD, the Romans built massive walls as part of their coastal fortifications in the English countryside, using water-worn flint cobbles. In the Middle Ages, cobblestone streets, houses and outbuildings were constructed throughout England and Europe. The technique was adapted and refined in the United States to become a uniquely American form of building construction. Settlers used stones gathered from fields to build fences and foundations for their buildings. Sometime between 1825 and 1830, an unknown mason built a house using smaller stones in horizontal courses. This design idea spread rapidly.[87]

The identity and location of the mason of the first cobblestone building remains a mystery. It is assumed, however, that he resided somewhere south of Lake Ontario. It is likely that the construction of cobblestone buildings began on farms and later migrated to villages, but it remained a predominantly rural construction method.[88]

There are major historic connections between the completion of the Erie Canal in 1825 and the advent of the cobblestone era. The Erie Canal created an economic boom. Farmers in the areas with easy access to the canal were becoming financially prosperous from the marketing of their wheat, flour and other cash crops on the Atlantic Seaboard. These farmers were now able to build houses reflecting this prosperity and their confidence in the future. This encouraged farmers to clear more land, necessitating the removal of the stones in these fields. A successful farmer wanted a "more showy" home; a cobblestone house was a logical option. It would be much more fireproof than a conventional wooden frame house. And the cobblestone house would give an air of "permanence." Paint was expensive, and a cobblestone house would be easier and cheaper to maintain. The building material—the cobblestones—was free and could be rather easily gathered from plowed fields or brought home in oxcarts after the delivery of wheat to ports such as Sodus Bay.[89]

The stone-gathering task was the responsibility of the future homeowner. Often, boys were paid ten cents a day to walk beside a stone boat to collect stones turned up from plowing. The stone-gathering could often take several years. The stones had to be sorted by size and, sometimes, by color. This was a job for children and women. Sometimes, there would be a neighborhood "bee" to sort the stones, followed by a big supper and then music and dancing.[90]

Common lore has it that the cobblestone building masons were formerly canal masons. As this story goes, these masons had been lured to the area to build the locks on the Erie Canal and, on completion of the canal, sought other work. They wanted to stay in the area, appreciating the beauty of the region and the reasonable land costs.[91] The reality is that the Erie Canal was such an economic success that the masons had plentiful follow-up work on the canal throughout all three cobblestone building periods. Specifically, a widening and deepening of the original Erie Canal began in 1832 and continued through 1862. Almost one-half of the cobblestone buildings were erected between 1836 and 1846, when the canal masons were employed in this canal work. The demand for masons on the canal was primarily for building locks and aqueducts. Over 65 percent of these structures were built east of Syracuse; only 4 percent of the cobblestone buildings are found east of Syracuse. The masonry for canal locks and aqueducts called for large blocks of stone, not small cobblestones. Interestingly, in Lockport, New York, where canal masons built a series of five locks to climb the Niagara escarpment, masons built their homes of cut stone blocks, not cobblestones! It also needs to be pointed out that some cobblestone buildings were erected as early as 1810—predating the start of Erie Canal construction in 1817, let alone its completion in 1825. Although some canal masons may have built cobblestone houses, it was probably local masons or even local farmers who learned the skills and built their own and their relatives' homes. An issue of the *Genesee Farmer* published a series of inquiries and responses from farmers asking about the process of cobblestone building. The responses say nothing about needing masonry skills or locating a skilled mason.[92]

The identities of the masons for most of the cobblestone buildings are not known. It is unlikely that they brought their skills from Europe, since the early cobblestone construction in the Greater Rochester area lagged by fifty years the skills shown in English construction. There must have been many masons for these cobblestone buildings, as there were a large number of such buildings constructed over a short period of time. It is believed that only a few masons built more than three or four cobblestone buildings. It is likely that many cobblestone houses were built by their owners, who learned the construction techniques by word of mouth or from their temporary work on the Erie Canal. The evolution of this building style during its three periods reveals an increasing skill and sophistication in the masonry.[93]

A good mason could lay four courses (about eighteen to twenty-four inches of wall) per day. The daily pay for a mason in 1850 was between $1.00 and $1.50, plus "board" for working a ten- to twelve-hour workday. Generally, only one mason worked on a building at a time. This would allow the necessary time for the mortar to begin to set. This also meant that it could take a season to complete the building, and in some cases as long as two or three years. A mason might work on two or three buildings concurrently per season. Each mason had his own style of selecting and assembling cobblestones. It is thus possible to determine that a particular cobblestone building and others nearby were likely erected by the same mason.[94]

A soft lime mortar was the glue that held the cobbles together. This mortar was made of lime, sand and water, but each mason tended to have his own unique recipe. The magic of soft lime mortar was that it cured slowly, letting the stones settle and bear weight. It could take up to thirty-five years for the mortar to fully harden—giving the building time to settle without cracking. It must be kept in mind that this era predated the use of Portland cement. The cobblestone buildings can't be repaired with modern mortar, which dries too hard and too fast and would push the cobblestones out.[95]

From the beginning, masons used stone quoins at the corners of the houses. Quoins are rectangular stones used to strengthen corners and to improve the appearance of the building. Initially, these were small stone blocks about two or three courses of cobblestones high. Later, masons used square stones twelve inches high, six to eight inches thick and sixteen to eighteen inches long. As the size of the stones selected became smaller, four courses, then five courses and, finally, six courses of stones were finished with a twelve-inch-high quoin at the corners.[96]

Limestone blocks and slabs for quoins (for structural strength at the corners of the building), sills and lintels could be easily and economically transported from area quarries. A sill is the horizontal piece at the bottom of a door or window opening; a lintel is the horizontal piece over a door or window that bears the weight of the structure above it. During the construction of the Erie Canal, quarries had been established at Albion, Geneva, LeRoy, Medina, Phelps and Rochester.[97]

The most distinctive feature of cobblestone buildings is their texture. Texture is determined by the size and composition of the cobblestones, by the mortar joint treatment and by the patterns created by mortar joints and cobblestones. Most cobblestone buildings feature smaller stones on the front and larger stones on the sides and rear. This can be immediately seen by counting the number of vertical cobblestone courses at the stone quoins. Closer inspection of the cobblestone wall will reveal an added dimension of artwork expressed in the mortar between the rows of stones. Since the cobbles are laid in horizontal course, the horizontal mortar joint is usually in the shape of a projecting V, with the point of the V forming a continuous horizontal line between courses. Occasionally, this horizontal joint has been finished with a beading trowel, which makes a continuous bead or half-round projection. This continuous line helps to bring order to what otherwise could be a random collection of stones. The desire for ornamentation led builders to exploit the inherent character of the stones in various ways. For example, sometimes, a herringbone pattern was achieved by laying the stones diagonally and reversing the direction in each successive row or course. Special effects could be achieved by the careful collection and sorting of water-rounded stones by color. The real beauty of cobblestone buildings depends on light. Without this, particularly sunlight, the texture of the stones and mortar joints is minimized, and the fascinating patterns recede. "Sunlight, raking across the textured surface, gives vibrancy to the building that is unique. Perhaps the most harmonious manifestation of man and nature in upstate New York is the rural cobblestone building dappled by sunlight and surrounded by open fields."[98]

Not only homes but also churches, schools and stores were constructed with cobblestones. In addition, an octagonal blacksmith shop in Alloway, a factory in Perry and a Masonic temple building in Pittsford were erected with cobblestones.[99] There were cobblestone barns, smokehouses, mills, carriage houses, gate- and tollhouses and privies. There was even at least one cobblestone tombstone (in Meridian, New York)!

Part B: Cobblestone Buildings in Seneca County

There are at least seventeen cobblestone structures still in use in Seneca County. Pioneer craftsmen in the middle third of the nineteenth century perfected a form of folk art—namely, the use of glacially rounded stones—that was without precedent in the country.[100] The short-lived cobblestone craft nevertheless had a long-lasting influence in the area. As mentioned earlier, Rich and Sue Freeman maintain that this artistic period represents the last generation of houses built entirely by hand.[101]

The Woodworth Cobblestone House (936 East Tyre Road, town of Tyre) was built in 1844. It consists of a two-story main section with a one-and-a-half-story wing to the west side. The basement has a fieldstone foundation and an old, curved, brick baking oven built into the chimney. The walls are a foot and a half thick; the cobbles themselves are random in color and size.[102]

The Lay Cobblestone House (1175 Old School House Road, town of Tyre) was built by Hiram Lay. The cobblestone barn just across the road to the north was demolished when the Montezuma National Wildlife Refuge acquired the property. The cupola from the barn was then placed on the roof of the house itself. The one-story porch at the entryway adds a Victorian note to the front of the house. There is a brick smokehouse

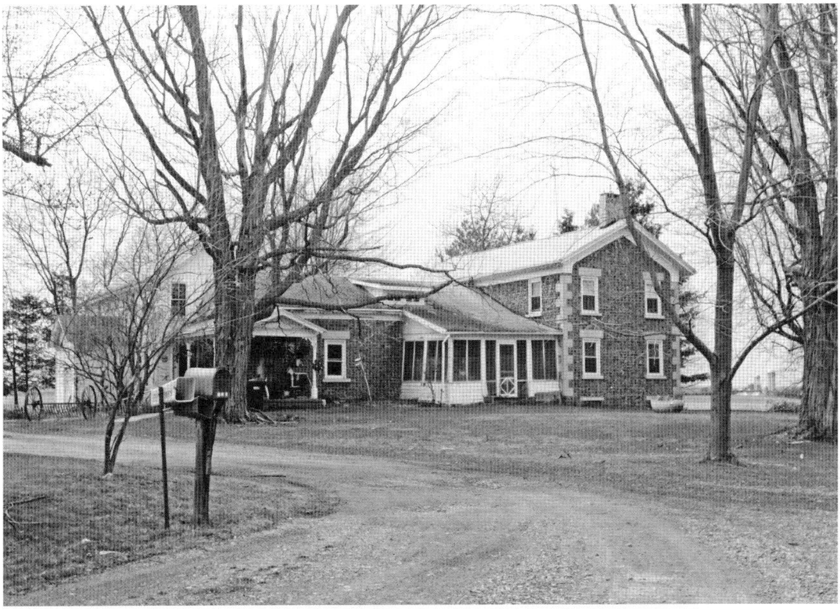

The walls of this cobblestone house (936 East Tyre Road, town of Tyre) are eighteen inches thick, with cobbles that are random in color and size. *Walter Gable.*

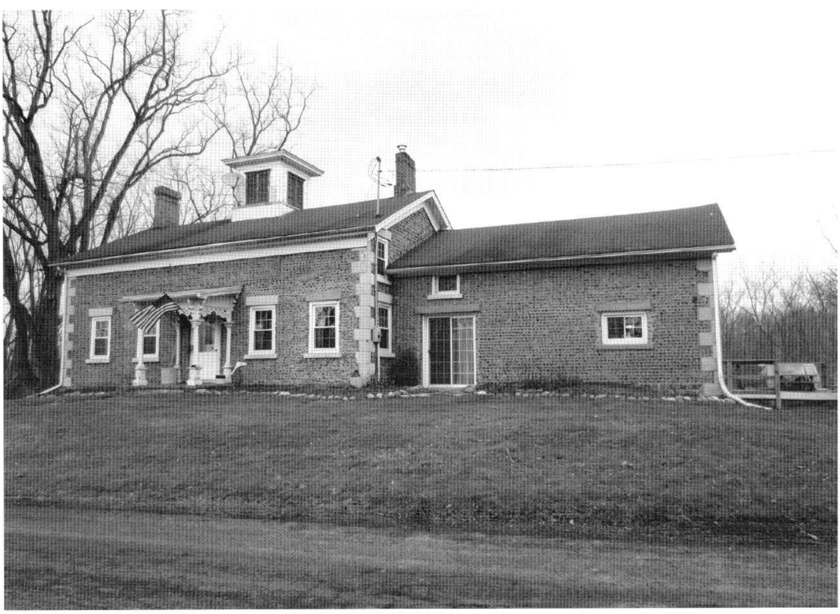

The cupola on this house (1175 Old School House Road, town of Tyre) actually was on the farm's cobblestone barn, torn down when the Montezuma National Wildlife Refuge was created. *Walter Gable.*

on the rear slope, and the house has an original baking oven built into an inside chimney wall.[103]

The Seekell Cobblestone House (1262 Gravel Road, town of Tyre) was built by early residents named Seekell. The house has wide floorboards, hand-cut beams and hand-laid foundations. The old door at the original front of the house has nine panes. Once a double house, it has an open stair at one side of the house and a closed and curved stair at the opposite end. Since the house was constructed in two phases, there are many walls now inside that were originally outside. An unusual feature of the windows is the trim on the inside, which tapers inward as it approaches the ceiling, so that the sill or lower part measures thirty inches, but the windows narrow to twenty-four inches at the top.[104]

A two-story, five-bay cobblestone house (1229 Birdsey Road, town of Junius) was built in the 1830s or 1840s in the Federal style. Built by three different workmen, it perfectly illustrates typical construction methods of

Opposite, top: The front side of this house (1229 Birdsey Road, town of Junius) reflects the Federal-style emphasis on symmetry and balance. *Walter Gable.*

Below: Note the distinctive quoins at the corners (1262 Gravel Road, town of Tyre). *Walter Gable.*

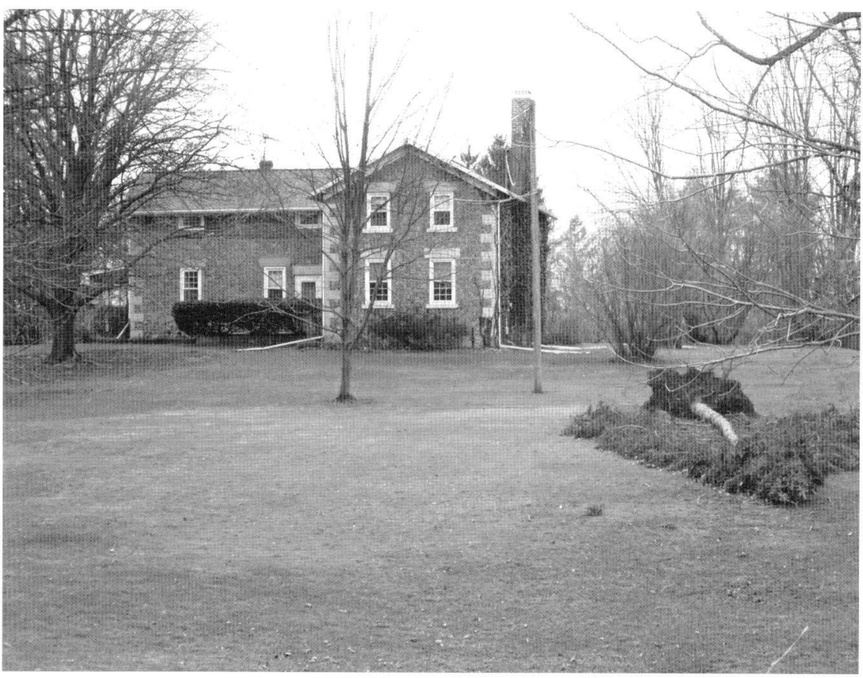

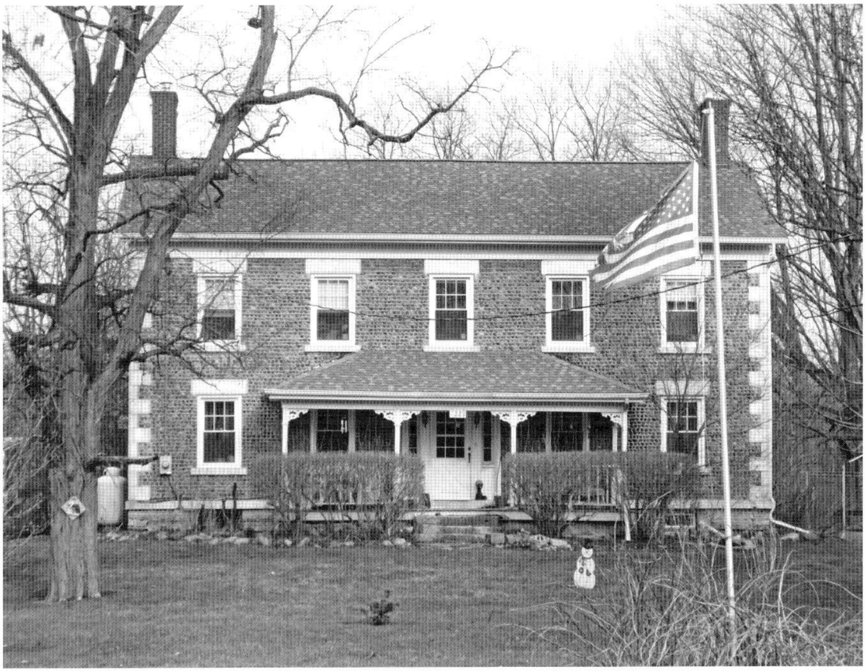

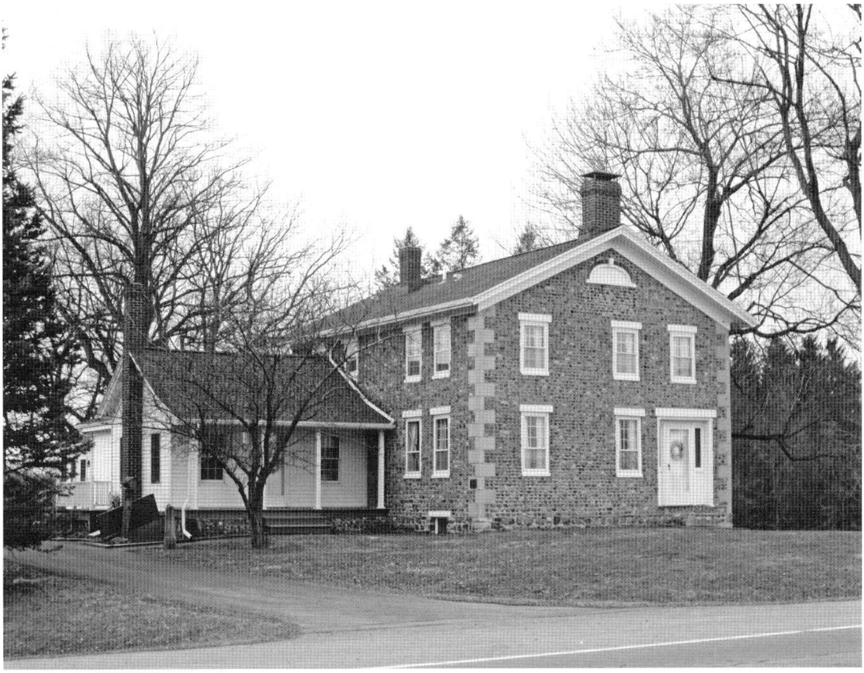

John Graves built this cobblestone house (1370 Route 318, town of Tyre) in 1837. *Walter Gable.*

the time. The back was done by an apprentice, with large stones set in lines that were far from straight. A journeyman then built the sides with smaller stones and straighter courses. The master mason built the front of the house using the smallest stones and presenting the home's most pleasing face to the road. There is a dirt floor in the basement, which once had a baking oven as part of the fireplace system. The basement features twin chimneys on the north and south sides. The house has walls twenty-four inches thick. There is a hand-dug well, a milk house and two barns.[105]

The Graves Cobblestone House (1370 Route 318, town of Junius) was built by John Graves in 1837. The two-story, three-bay home has four rooms downstairs and three rooms and a bath upstairs, with an open staircase to the second floor and a fireplace in the parlor. A wide overhang is formed by the roof and fan windows in the gables.[106]

A cobblestone church (corner of Stone Church Road and Route 318, town of Junius) was constructed in 1839 as a Methodist Episcopal church. It has a wide entablature and small returns, with a large, oval stained-glass window on the gable end. There was once a wooden porch

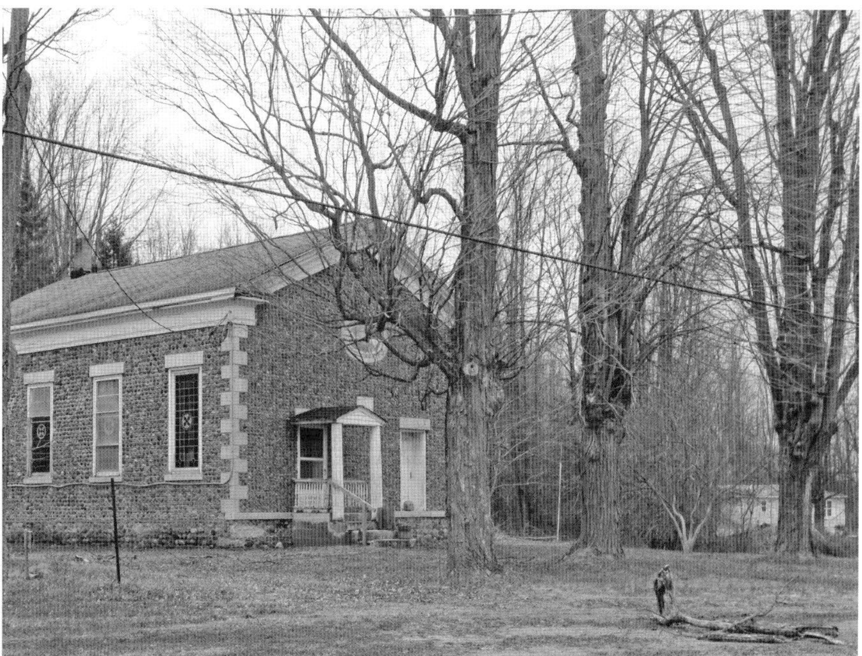

Although today a private residence, this building (1434 Old State Road Extension, town of Tyre) was constructed in 1839 as a Methodist Episcopal church. *Walter Gable.*

that extended across the front of the church, which had wooden steps on all three sides. The building served as a church until 1969, when it became a private home.[107]

The Federal-style Holmes House (1111 Stone Church Road, town of Junius) was built of stones from nearby fields between 1820 and 1824. It is five bays wide and has a long cobblestone addition stretching to the south. All of the windows have stone lintels and sills, the lintels being ten and a half inches thick and the sills four and a half inches. The courses of the house are four to the quoin, except for those on the north wall of the house and the south wall of the wing, where they are three courses to the quoin. All the quoins are made of squared limestone. There are two fireplaces in this house: a brick fireplace in the family room and a stone fireplace in the living room. Downstairs are seven rooms and a full bath; upstairs are four rooms and a bathroom. The basement is the same size as the house; a former owner kept his cattle there.[108]

The Gassner Farm cobblestone house (1079 Stone Church Road, town of Junius) was built in the 1830s and '40s in the Federal style. Because it so closely resembles another cobblestone structure on the same road to the south, it may have had the same builder. A local resident who lived here as a child reports that the wing projecting to the south housed a woodshed. The

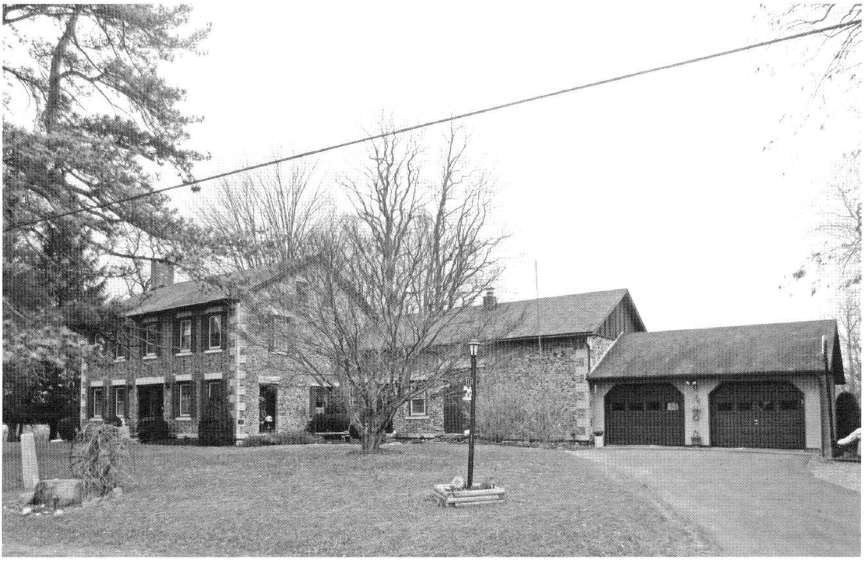

The original portion of this house (1111 Stone Church Road, town of Tyre) was built between 1820 and 1824 using stones from nearby fields. *Walter Gable.*

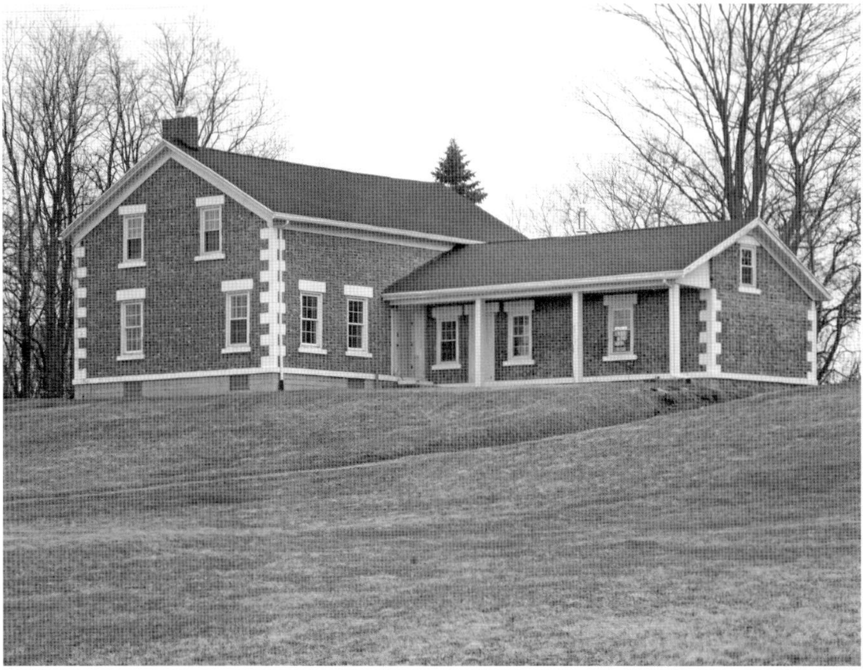

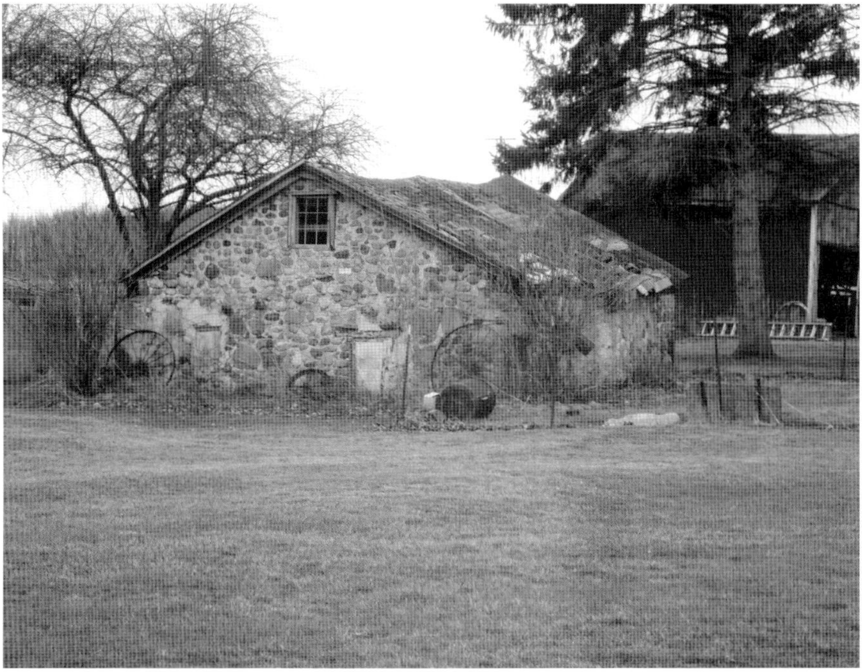

wooden door in the upper section of this gable served as the opening into which wood was thrown. For many years, the basement was dirt-floored to help keep the food stored there cool.[109]

The stone barn built by the Lundy family (465 Garrett Road, town of Junius) was and is one of the few stone barns still existing in Seneca County. The barn was originally used for hogs, which went in and out of the small door. The barn is of additional interest because of the extreme variation in color and size of its stones, ranging from cobbles to boulders, all probably collected from the area. The small door has a heavy wooden beam for a lintel; another heavy wooden beam supports the roof.[110]

The Carman Cobblestone House (533 Dublin Road, town of Junius), was constructed in the Greek Revival style in the 1840s or 1850s. One of

Opposite, top: The quoins, water table and window lintels and sills have been painted white (1079 Stone Church Road, town of Tyre). *Walter Gable.*

Opposite, bottom: A few cobblestone barns were built in Seneca County, but this is the only known surviving one. *Walter Gable.*

Below: Although many cobblestone houses were built in the Federal style, this one (533 Dublin Road, town of Junius) has many Greek Revival features. *Walter Gable.*

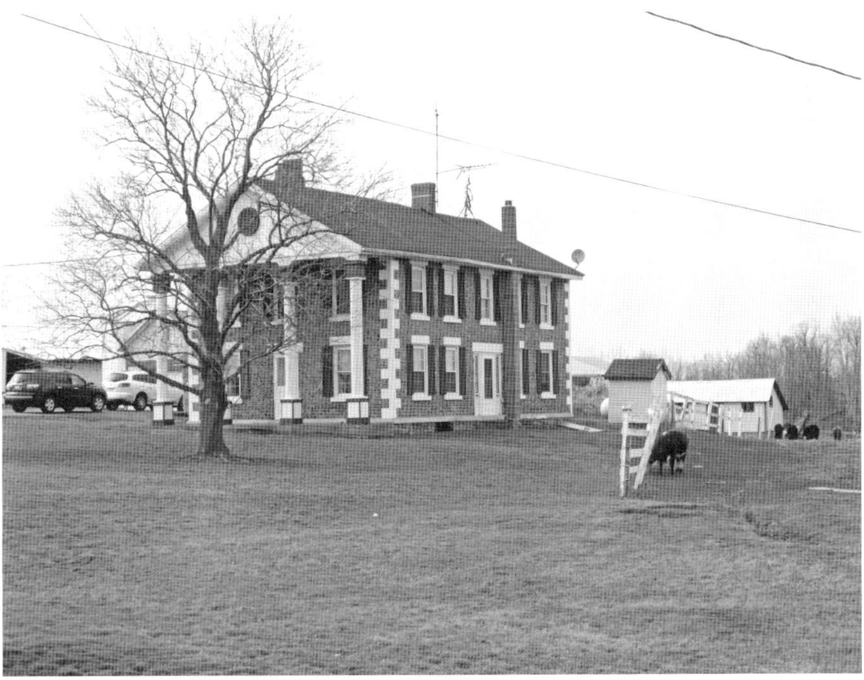

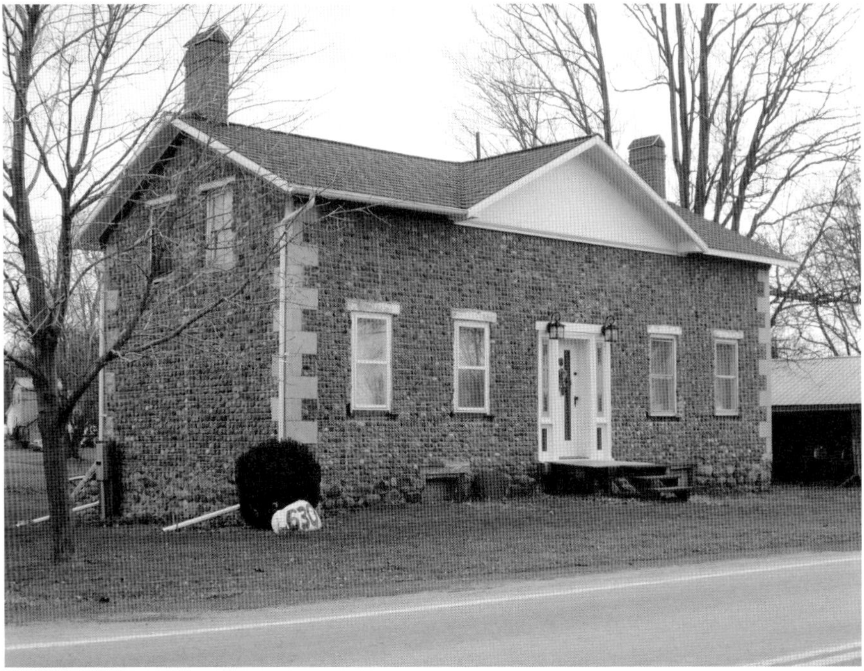

Above: It is encouraging to see recent owners of cobblestone buildings making efforts to maintain these unique structures (630 Dublin Road, town of Junius). *Walter Gable.*

Opposite, top: This structure (2523 Lower Lake Road, Seneca Falls) was built in 1830 by Julius Bull, who also erected a similar cobblestone house in the town of Varick. *Walter Gable.*

the largest in the county, it has a bell on the roof housed in a cobblestone addition. The classical front columns are set on square bases of a different color. An unusual round window in the large pediment faces the road. The house was built by John Carman.[111]

There is a small cobblestone house at 630 Dublin Road in the town of Junius. Recent owners have been restoring much of the exterior.

The Ferry Farm Cobblestone House (2523 Lower Lake Road, town of Seneca Falls) was constructed in 1830 by Julius Bull. The structure faces Cayuga Lake. Both the house and its property have had an interesting history. The first ferry across Cayuga Lake was operated from a landing here, until a bridge was constructed in 1800. The house was originally used as a tavern, and it is locally believed to have served as a station on the Underground Railroad. A symmetrical, five-bay house built in the Federal style, it has stone lintels and sills, and there is a semi-elliptical fan window in each of the two gables of the main wing.[112]

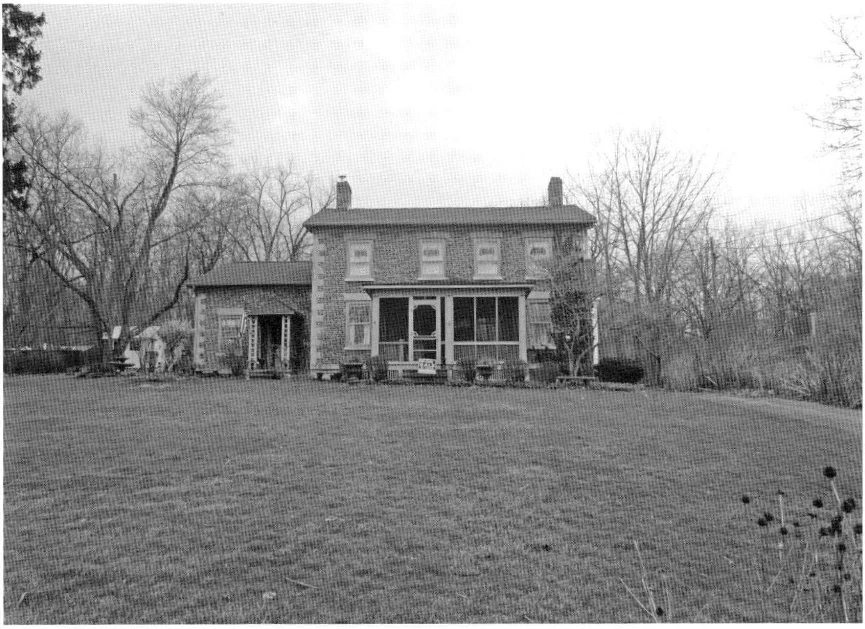

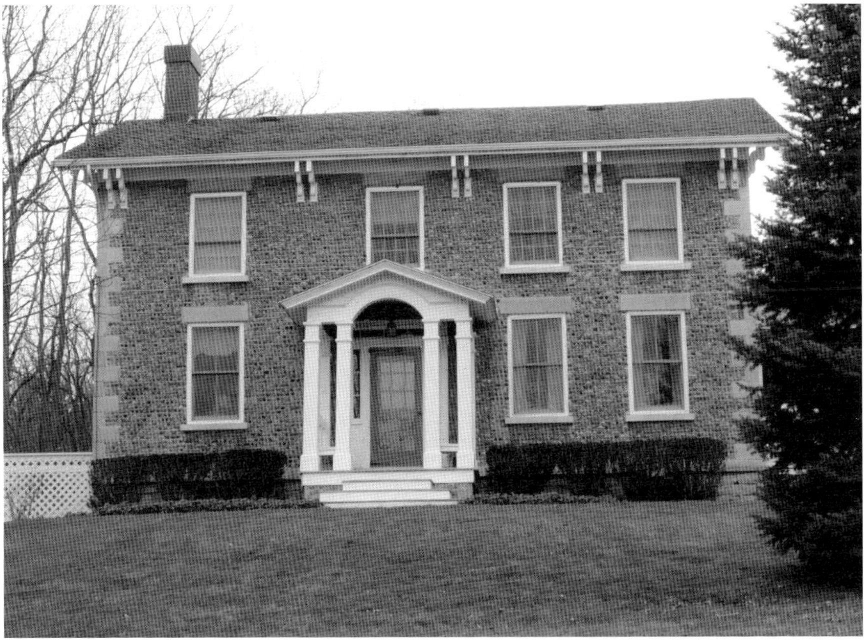

Located in the town of Varick, this (5102 Route 89) was a second cobblestone house built by Julius Bull. *Walter Gable.*

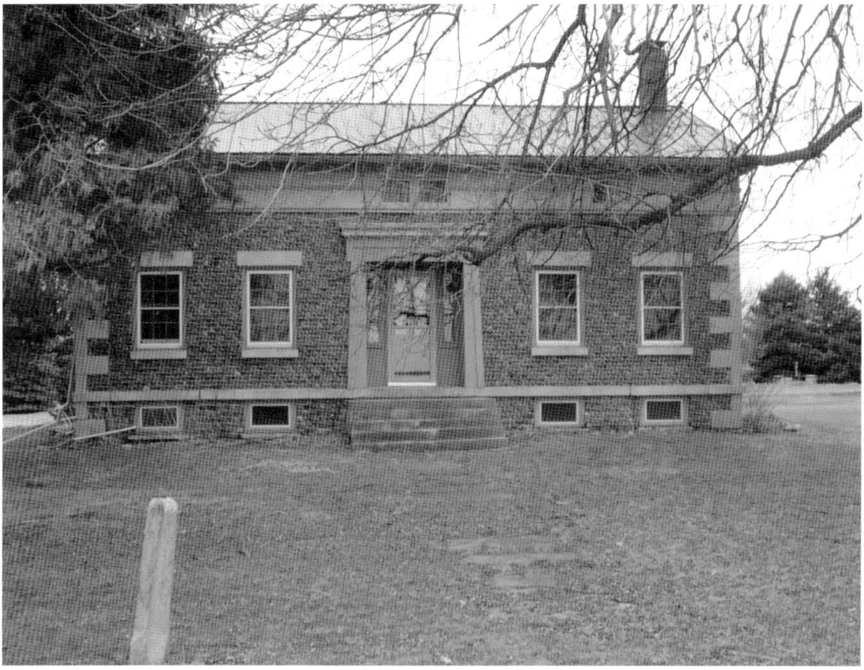

Above: Note the indented front entry, the distinctive water sill and the frieze windows on the front side facing Ritter Road (3333 Ritter Road, town of Fayette). *Walter Gable.*

Opposite, top: Note the side entry, which has a much cruder appearance than the main structure in terms of the quoins and nature of the cobbles (543 Bedell Road, town of Junius). *Walter Gable.*

Opposite, bottom: A recent owner painted the original cobblestone wall white, apparently to match the wooden siding of the addition (1515 O'Dell Road, town of Junius). *Walter Gable.*

A cobblestone house built by Julius Bull in 1833 (5102 Route 89, town of Varick) is a simple rectangular building, with four downstairs rooms with a central hall and four rooms upstairs. In the 1980s, the George Souhan family added an extensive three-bedroom wing to the west and an outdoor patio to the south. Three well-preserved barns remain from an earlier time, as does the boathouse across the road.[113]

A cobblestone house in the town of Fayette (3333 Ritter Road, on the corner of Aunkst Road) has beautiful quoins at the corners and a distinctive water sill. The front entry is indented. The front side facing Ritter Road has several small frieze windows.

At some point, an owner of the Hicks House (1515 O'Dell Road, town of Junius) tried to paint the cobblestones on the east side, which doesn't directly face the road.

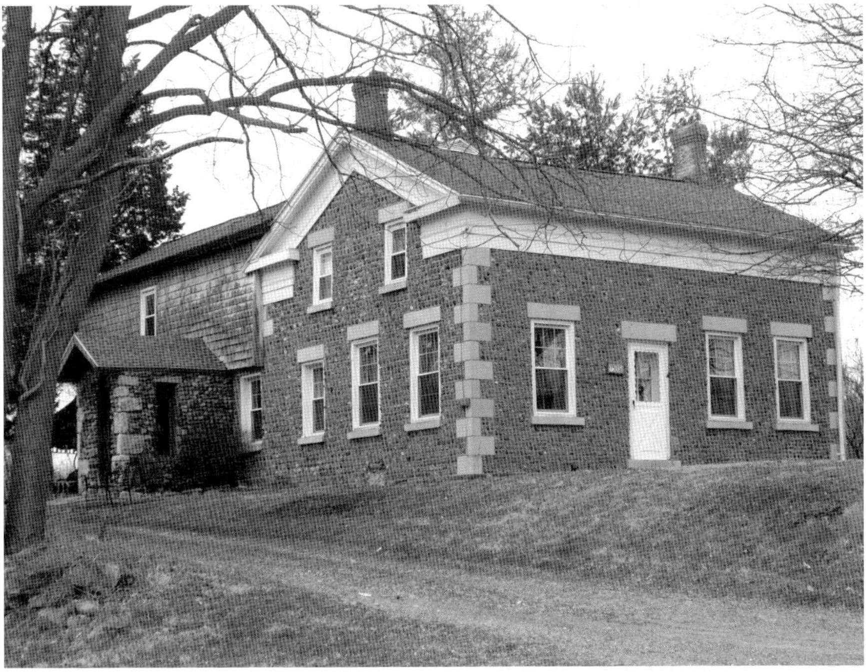

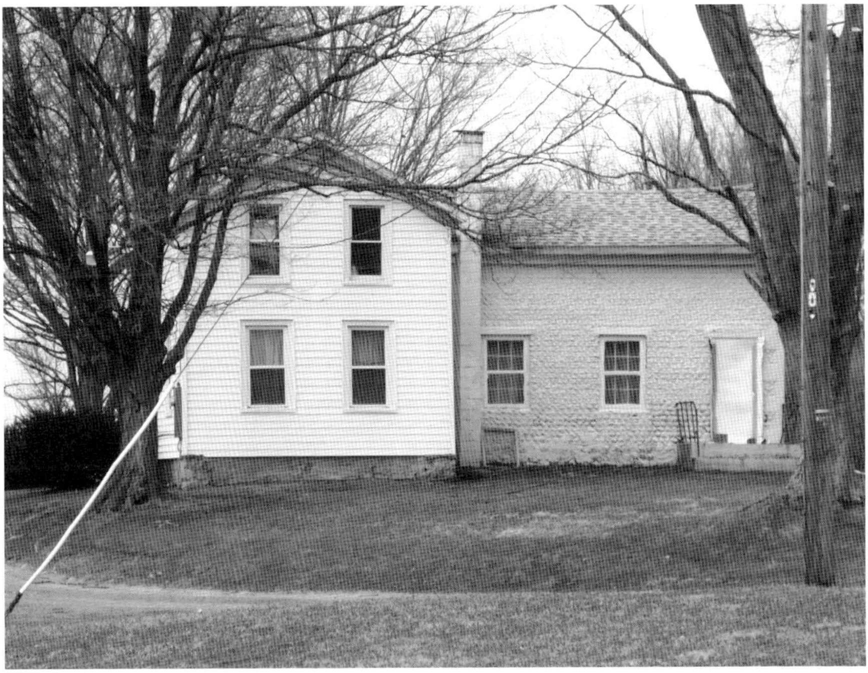

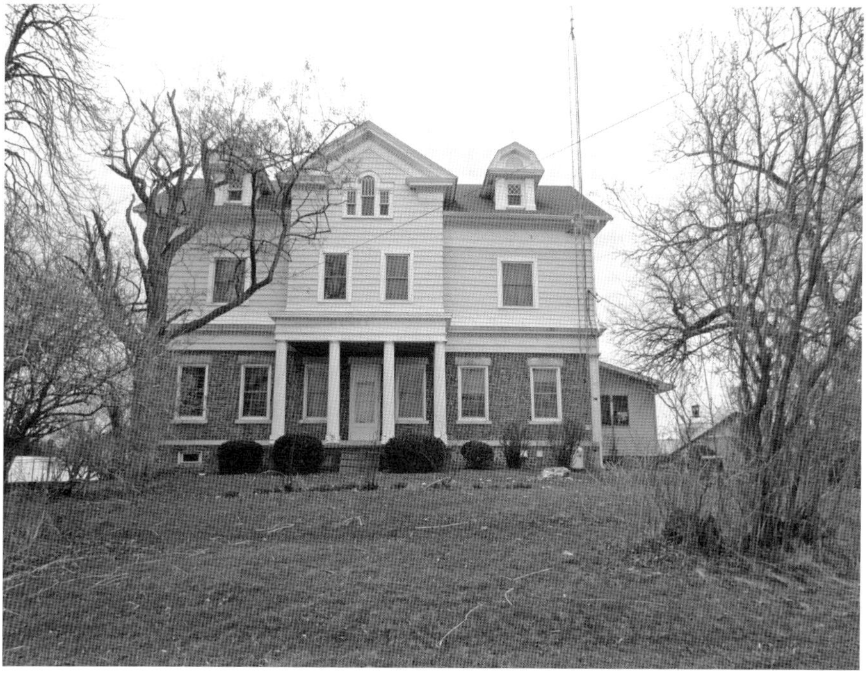

Originally a one-and-a-half-story cobblestone house, this structure (3792 Post Road, town of Fayette) had a roof raised, with the wooden portion reflecting later building styles. *Walter Gable.*

The Nearpass House (543 Bedell Road, town of Junius) shows how an original cobblestone home is often added on to make a larger residence. In this case, the additions are wooden. The entrance door is placed to the right rather than centered on that side of the original cobblestone structure. Cut limestone blocks made up the steps and landing to this entry door.

In one case, an original cobblestone house (3792 Post Road, town of Fayette) was "enlarged" by raising the roof to add wooden stories. The wooden portion reflects many qualities of building styles that arose later than those used in the original construction. For many years, the "ballroom" on the top floor was a gathering place for entertaining local farm families.

Conclusion

Interest in cobblestone structures tapered off as labor costs increased. Cobblestone construction was very labor intensive, and the advent of steam-powered sawmills and the availability of wood from Pennsylvania and the Adirondacks lowered the cost of construction with timber.[114]

Although some of the cobblestone houses have been lost, most of those still standing benefit from owners who appear to be maintaining them properly. These structures are certainly worthy of being preserved. Rochester architect Claude Bragdon referred to the cobblestone era as "evidence of our architectural Golden Age." In his opinion, "Austere and humble as these buildings are, they show a beauty and integrity of a kind which made this country great, and should serve as inspiration to us today."[115]

8
William Watts Folwell

Near Sampson State Park on Route 96A is a historic marker honoring William Watts Folwell. He is known for being the first president of the University of Minnesota and writing an extensive history of the state of Minnesota. He is also credited, along with Henry Philip Tappan, the president of the University of Michigan, with popularizing the idea of junior colleges.[116] This chapter focuses on descriptions of Folwell's youth in the town of Romulus, providing the reader with some insight into what farm life was like in the three decades prior to the Civil War.

William Folwell was born on February 2, 1833, the son of Thomas Jefferson and Joanna (Bainbridge) Folwell.[117] His birthplace and childhood home was located on a 150-acre farm about two miles west of the Village of Romulus. The house was a simple one, white, with one main room and two more small ones in a lean-to, with three rooms upstairs. The farm had the usual chickens, geese, turkeys, pigs and many fruit trees.[118]

From his memoirs, we get an idea of what William's life was like growing up on that farm. He said that he did the work typical of a boy on a farm at the time. This included carrying the mail some three miles to and from the post office, turning the grindstone handle or the handle of the fanning mill, cutting and carrying wood and tending the garden. Three of his early childhood recollections bear special mention. First, he was caught up in the enthusiasm of the "Tippecanoe and Tyler, Too" campaign slogan in the 1840 presidential election. Second, at the age of ten, he accompanied his uncle on horseback the sixty miles to Avon and then rode home alone.

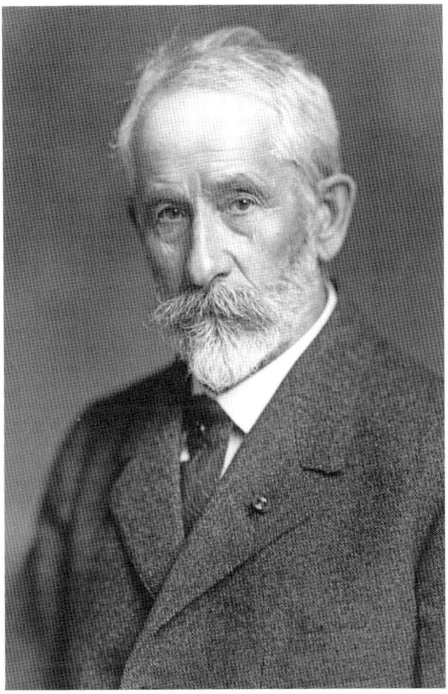

This is a 1921 photo of William Watts Folwell, the first president of the University of Minnesota. *Minnesota Historical Society.*

His third childhood recollection is especially noteworthy. His first formal education was at a summer school session. At that time, there was no general taxation for public education, and each school district pretty much operated as it wished. William's schoolhouse was fairly primitive. On three sides of the room there was a sloping shelf that took the place of desks. The younger children gathered nearer the center of the room, not far from the stove. There was one small blackboard. The emphasis was on the three Rs; there were no real grades.

Demonstrating academic ability, William went to live with his uncle and aunt in Nunda, New York, so that he could attend the Nunda Literary Institute. To get there, he traveled on the railroad from Geneva to Rochester, then by packet boat on the Genesee Canal to Mount Morris. Finally, he rode eleven miles in a four-horse stagecoach to Nunda. He went to this school for two years, but he spent his summers at his Romulus home.

Community life in Romulus at this time still had many of the "older customs," such as "raising of buildings," the Singing School and games of "one ole cat" and "two ole cat." William's family was Baptist, and there were two services (one-half hour apart) on Sunday at the Baptist Meeting House and congregational baptisms in nearby Seneca Lake. "The use of liquor was almost universal. Elder Caton, who preached at the Baptist Meeting House, would sometimes stop in his discourse to refresh himself with a small sip.… Any caller at a home must be offered some liquor—the minister most surely of all." William encountered the Washingtonian Temperance Movement while attending school at Nunda.

Up to this time, clothing and other goods were produced in the home from materials grown on the farm. Then came the advent of factories,

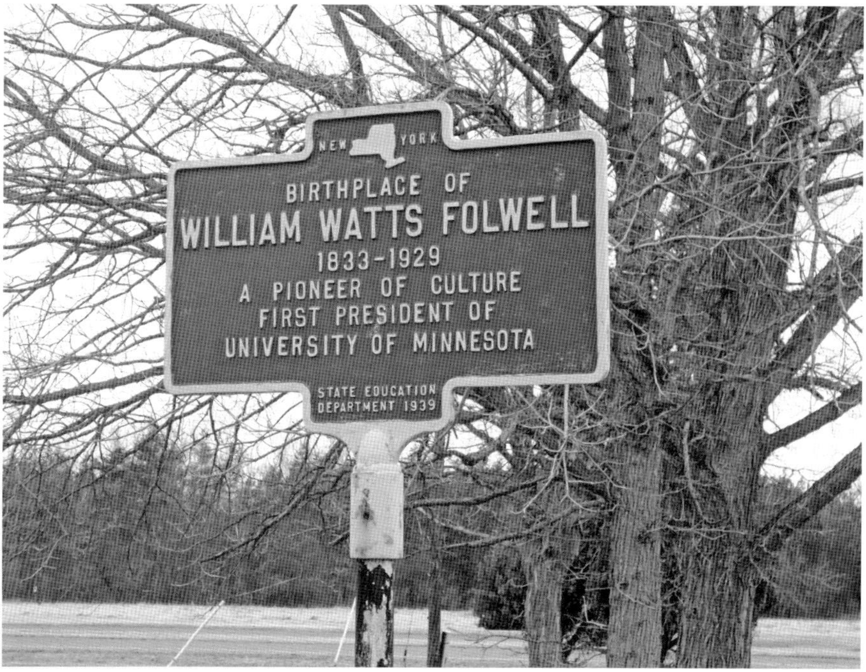

Folwell was born on a farm near present-day Sampson State Park in the town of Romulus. *Walter Gable.*

among them Woolen Mills at Waterloo and Seneca Falls, which were opened in the 1840s. Farm families would take wool to the factory and exchange it for finished cloth. The cloth was then taken to a tailor to be cut out; the sewing and finishing were done at home, often by "tailoresses" who went from house to house.

A similar transformation was taking place in terms of tools on the farm. For years, farm implements were of a crude, homemade variety. They were replaced by manufactured ones of far better design and finish. The first harvesting machines came in 1850. Improvements in plows and harvest machinery made farm labor much less burdensome and more efficient.

After his two years at the Nunda school, William went to the Geneva Union School. Feeling that the teaching there was poor, his family had him transferred to a private Latin school in Geneva. Following a small crop harvest, however, there was not enough cash for the family to pay for William's continued study. He became a teacher at a district school in Middlesex. "He needed little in the way of special preparation for this work, but his father, who held on to some old ideas strongly, insisted that William must have a silk hat to support the dignity of a schoolmaster, and so presented him with one—at the expense of four dollars." William earned fifty-six dollars for three months of teaching.

The next step in William's education took place at the Ovid Academy. Here, he had thorough training in Greek and other subjects and began his study of German. In his second year of study, the family rented the Purdy house in Ovid so that William's brother, two sisters and some cousins could attend the academy.

William went to Hobart Free College in Geneva, which offered him free tuition. Much to his surprise, he entered as a sophomore. In his last year at this college, he was also teaching Greek and Latin at the Ovid Academy and tutoring his brother two hours a day. Despite this strenuous workload, William graduated as valedictorian of his class at Hobart in 1857. Following college graduation, he taught at the Seneca Collegiate Institute, the new name for the former Ovid Academy, in 1857–58. He became an adjunct professor at Hobart, first teaching math and then foreign languages. He traveled in Europe in 1860 and 1861 but returned home to serve in the Fiftieth Engineers in the Civil War.[119]

Following stints in business and then teaching math at Kenyon College, William Folwell became, at the age of thirty-six, the first president of the University of Minnesota. At that time, there was only one building on campus; the library held only sixteen volumes. He built up the college, serving as president until 1884. Folwell's visionary "Minnesota Plan" encompassed all levels of education, from elementary and secondary through higher education. The University of Minnesota offered college courses as well as graduate and professional programs.[120] His vision also intended the university to be a cultural center, with museums and a library. He was president of the Minneapolis Park Commission from 1895 to 1903. After that, he wrote an extensive history of the state of Minnesota.[121]

William Watts Folwell died in 1929 at the age of ninety-six. In his life, we see a Seneca County person who went on to greatness outside of this state. We also see in his memoirs what it was like to grow up on a farm in Seneca County in the 1830s and 1840s.

9

Brook Farm Barn

At the north edge of the Village of Interlaken stands the Brook Farm barn (also known as the Usher-Hunt barn), one of the few remaining Wells barns with the original slate roof completely intact. The Brook Farm barn was constructed in 1908 by Fred R. Usher. Its enduring beauty is a reminder of a past era.

John Wells Sr. began his building career in 1871 at the age of twenty-eight. In 1888, he filed for a patent for an improved wooden truss design for buildings and bridges that would combine simplicity and strength without the use of steel braces. Cross-section pieces of lumber were nailed and bolted together to make trusses. Usually, the trusses consisted of lumber measuring two inches by three inches by ten feet that were laminated and curved into an arch. Designed to strengthen the barn, these trusses also protected against wind and the outward pressure of hay stored in the barn. This truss structure made it possible for the center of the barn to be open—without standing support columns—allowing wagons to swing around and drive out. Typically, a hay track ran down the center of the barn, allowing the unloading of hay or straw from the wagons drawn to the mow by horses. Another trademark of a Wells barn was the window that had "lazy W trim molding." Most Wells barns were built in Monroe and Livingston Counties, with some in the Southern Tier, Interlaken, the Hudson River Valley and Granville. The last Wells barn was built in 1942. As many as forty-nine of these barns are still standing.

The Usher-Hunt, Brook Farm barn, constructed in 1908, measures forty feet by one hundred feet. The slate for the roof was quarried from the

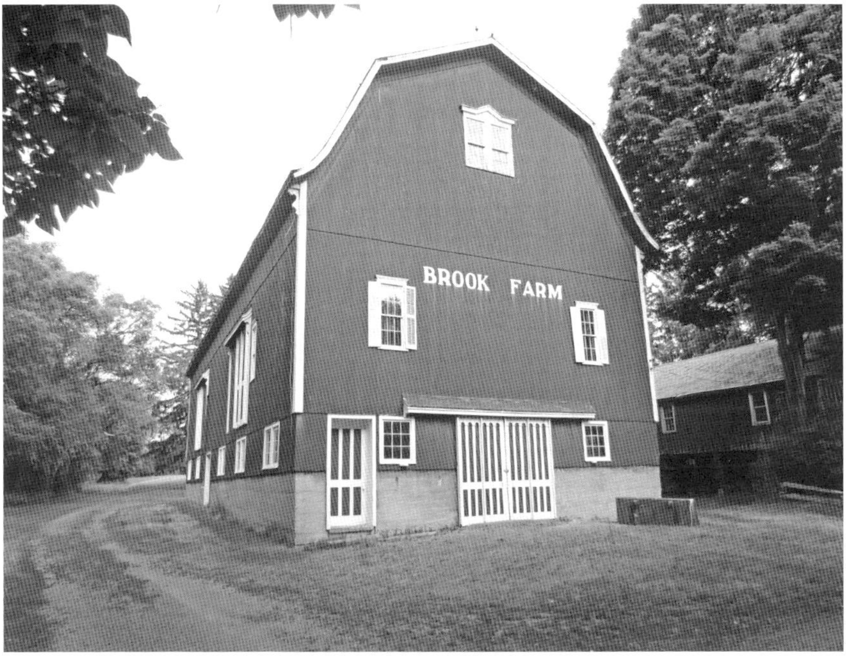

The Brook Farm barn in Interlaken is one of the few remaining Wells barns with an original slate roof. It was constructed in 1908. *Walter Gable.*

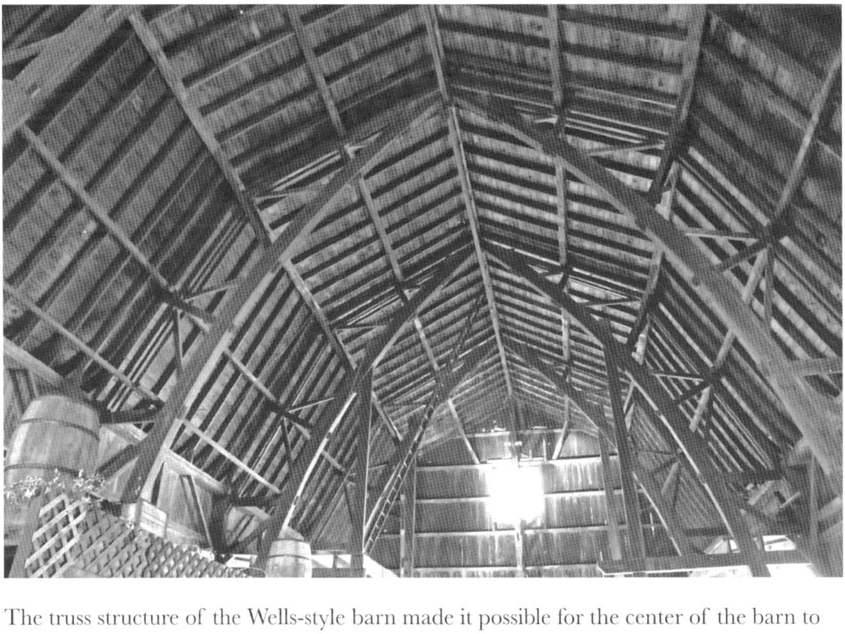

The truss structure of the Wells-style barn made it possible for the center of the barn to be open, without standing support columns. *Walter Gable.*

Norton Slate Quarry in Granville, New York, and shipped to Interlaken by railroad.[122] Granville is a town on the eastern border of Washington County, near the Vermont border. It has been called the "Colored Slate Capital of the World."[123] Reportedly, the quarry was owned by Herbert Usher's grandmother, who lived in Granville. Large hay chutes were built into the wall with hinged access doors at several levels. Smaller boxed-in ventilation units run from the basement to the eaves. The granaries stand on the south side of the main floor.

The basement of this barn is perhaps one of the first poured-concrete foundations in the area. The concrete floor has both gutters and curved mangers. The manger could be flooded with water for the cows, using a spring above the farm. This spring also cooled the milk in the milk house. (The 1935 flood destroyed much of this spring-fed water supply.) Originally, the floors were wooden planks over concrete, where the cows and horses stood.

Two of the original horse stalls can still be seen in the basement. The mangers, salt licks and combination sliding and Dutch doors are original. Across from the stalls is a small tack room.

The carriage house adjacent to the barn housed chickens and served as a run-in shed for the cows. Both the carriage house and the main barn have a unique curved design at the top of the sliding doors. The milk house and the smokehouse still stand south of the barn.[124]

Herbert Usher, who had this barn built, led an interesting life. He was a construction superintendent on the project to put the Waldorf and Astoria Hotels together in New York City. He retired shortly after that project was finished and moved to Interlaken to become a gentleman farmer.[125] According to Naomi Brewer, the barn was built by Fred R. Usher.[126]

The Usher family owned the property until 1950. It was then sold to the Cronk Dairy Company and then to the Hunt family. It is currently owned by John and Grace Hunt.[127]

10

Ku Klux Klan Activity Near Waterloo and Geneva in the 1920s

Was the Ku Klux Klan active in the Finger Lakes region in the 1920s? The answer is "yes." Although its work was often done in secret, some information can be uncovered and reported. The KKK of the 1920s capitalized on xenophobia and racism, opposing anyone who was not seen as "100% American": Catholics, Jews, rumrunners, immigrants, Bolsheviks, African Americans and other minority groups. In 1923, the *New York Times* estimated that there were 200,000 Klan members in New York State.[128]

Years ago, I heard stories of a KKK rally that took place on Sweets Hill in the 1920s, with thousands attending. Sweets Hill, in the town of Fayette, is about four miles south of the Village of Waterloo and just east of Route 96. It is the highest natural geographic point in northern Seneca County. As Seneca County historian, I wanted to write a story of this incident. I began searching for information in earnest in September 2013. I wasn't getting very far, and then, almost miraculously, while searching the Internet, I ran across a little article in the *Naples (NY) Record* of September 15, 1926. The article read as follows, in its entirety: "The Ku Klux Klan held a three day meeting four miles southwest of Waterloo, on what is known as Sweet's hill, Saturday, Sunday and Monday last. Fully 1500 Klansmen were gathered in the tented city, despite the inclement weather.–Waterloo News." Significantly, I was not able to find any local newspaper report on this gathering.

John Genung's research work on the KKK in the Waterloo area does reveal several local KKK rallies, including at places near Sweets Hill. One such event occurred in 1924 on the Raymond

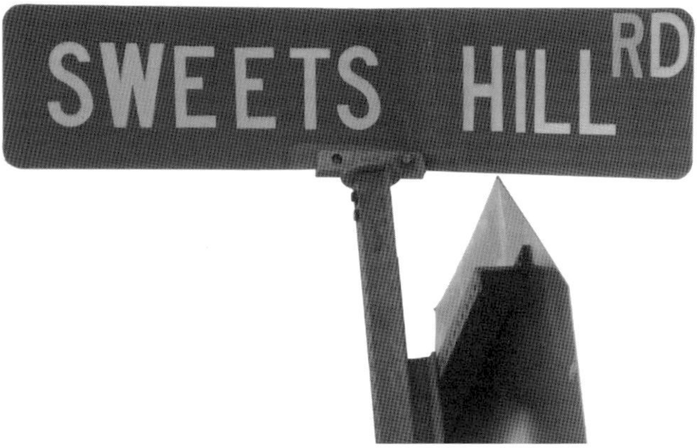

Sweets Hill was the site of a three-day KKK rally in September 1926, attended by 1,500 people. *Walter Gable.*

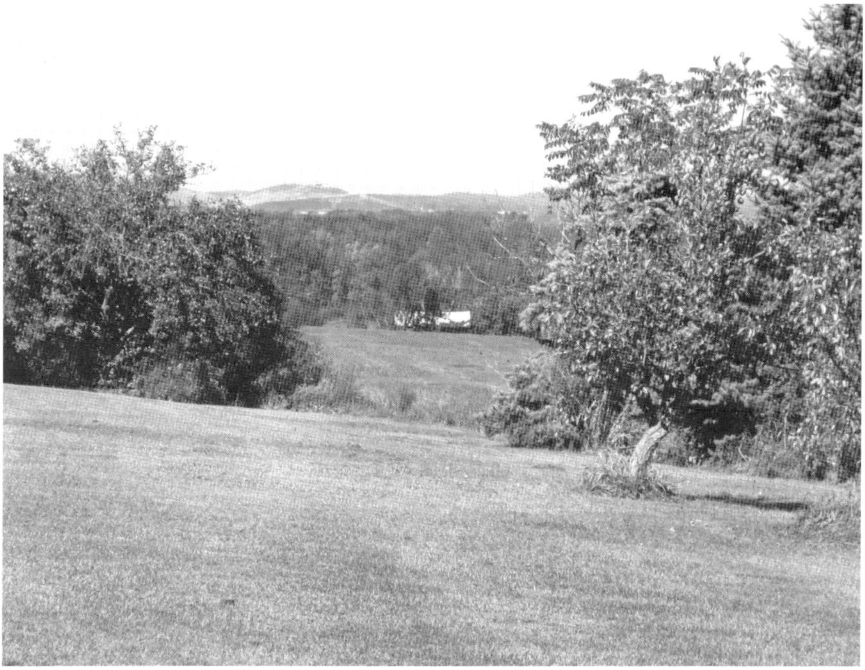

People from miles around could have seen the burning cross of the September 1926 KKK rally from this hill. *Walter Gable.*

Schaffer Sr. farm on the west side of Route 96 South, a bit north of County House Road and south of Shannon Drive. The gathering took place in a narrow open field between two small patches of woods. In that small field, the Klan "burned a fiery cross," according to Genung's report of Tom Boyes's telling of the story on July 4, 1993. Although Boyes was only four years old at the time of the incident, he said that he remembered it well, as it was quite an impressive event.[129]

Genung wrote that "during the 20s and probably the early 30s the local chapter of the KKK held Klan rallies or meetings in several places." He wrote that a cross was burned on the C.M. farm (he used initials rather than full names), on the north side of Routes 5 and 20, east of the Packwood Road. He reported that some law officers attempted to stop the rally and cross-burning. C.M. told the law officers to leave, "as he would do as he pleased on his land." Genung also wrote that at least one meeting—and maybe more than one—was held in the woods east of the Yost Road and west of Disinger Road, on the G.W. farm (not far from Sweets Hill).

Another incident that Genung described occurred sometime between 1923 and 1928. A mother and daughter were driving on Route 96 South, approaching Brown's Corners (Route 96 and County Road 121). It was near dark. A white-clad man arose from a ditch bank and waved the car to a stop. He asked the ladies if they were "looking for the meeting." They responded, "No" and were waved on. They were, however, scared stiff, fearing they were about to be murdered!

Genung also touched on a couple of things his father—an undertaker—told him about Ku Klux Klan happenings. Local Klan members called more than once to request the loan of folding chairs for a meeting. "After being assured that some were available," Genung wrote, "the caller would then indicate they were for the KKK. Possibly feeling a bit 'trapped,' Dad would indicate chairs could be borrowed by anyone as long as they were cared for and returned promptly. The caller would then say that a local trucker would be contacted to pick up, deliver and return the chairs. Arrangements were thus made in this manner. The chairs were always returned." Genung's father also described an incident in the early 1930s when the daughter of an alleged KKK member died. "A nice spray of flowers was sent to the family home where the funeral was held. The card on this floral arrangement read simply 'KKK.'"

A relative of Genung had a conversation with a local carpenter regarding the nature of a cross that was burned at a local Klan rally. The partially burned remnants revealed a well-constructed cross, indicating "professional work on the part of the builder. The man smiled but would neither confirm nor deny his involvement in the matter."

A final noteworthy account from Genung refers to his remembering that some intruder or "spy" was caught lurking in the woods around the fringes of a Klan meeting by guards or sentinels. He was threatened, perhaps roughed up a bit and then released. He hastened away from the rally meeting.[130]

Some specific information does exist regarding Ku Klux Klan activity in the Geneva area. A large KKK gathering was planned for October 10, 1925. The headquarters site was a large field on the Fordon Farm, just west of the city. A large tent had been erected on the field, a former airport, and a number of smaller tents were set up to serve various purposes. The rally did not materialize as expected, because an early autumn storm on the night of October 9 "of near blizzard proportions, swept down upon the city and literally put the Klansmen to rout." The *Geneva Times* described the event as follows:

> *It was a cold reception that Geneva gave the Klan today. Flurries of snow and blustering winds swept across the Fordon Farm where the Klan assembly was held. Klansmen who braved the weather wore anything from heavy sweaters to winter overcoats and earlaps. Some of the smaller tents blew down as fast as they were erected. The big tent held firm until a big blast of wind toppled the tent just as Klansmen were eating their lunch. Fortunately, no one was injured, but attempts to get the tent up again were unsuccessful. Officials in charge of the affair were much discouraged and were considering calling off the scheduled events, including the parade and fireworks that night. Although not as many Klansmen showed up as planned, there was a large delegation from Buffalo. Bands present were the Klan band from Elmira and the Tyre City Band from Seneca County. The fireworks did not get set off, but there are conflicting reports as to whether or not a small version of the planned parade actually took place.*[131]

This was not the only KKK gathering to take place in the Geneva area in the 1920s. A three-day "konclave" was held at the Klan encampment near Flint in early September 1927. Every member of the Geneva Police Department was put on duty for the Saturday, September 3 parade through the downtown business section of Geneva.[132] Between two hundred and three hundred Klansmen, including several women and children, participated in the parade, most arriving in automobiles from the camp at Flint. The parade formed on Washington Street, west of Pulteney Street. The procession was

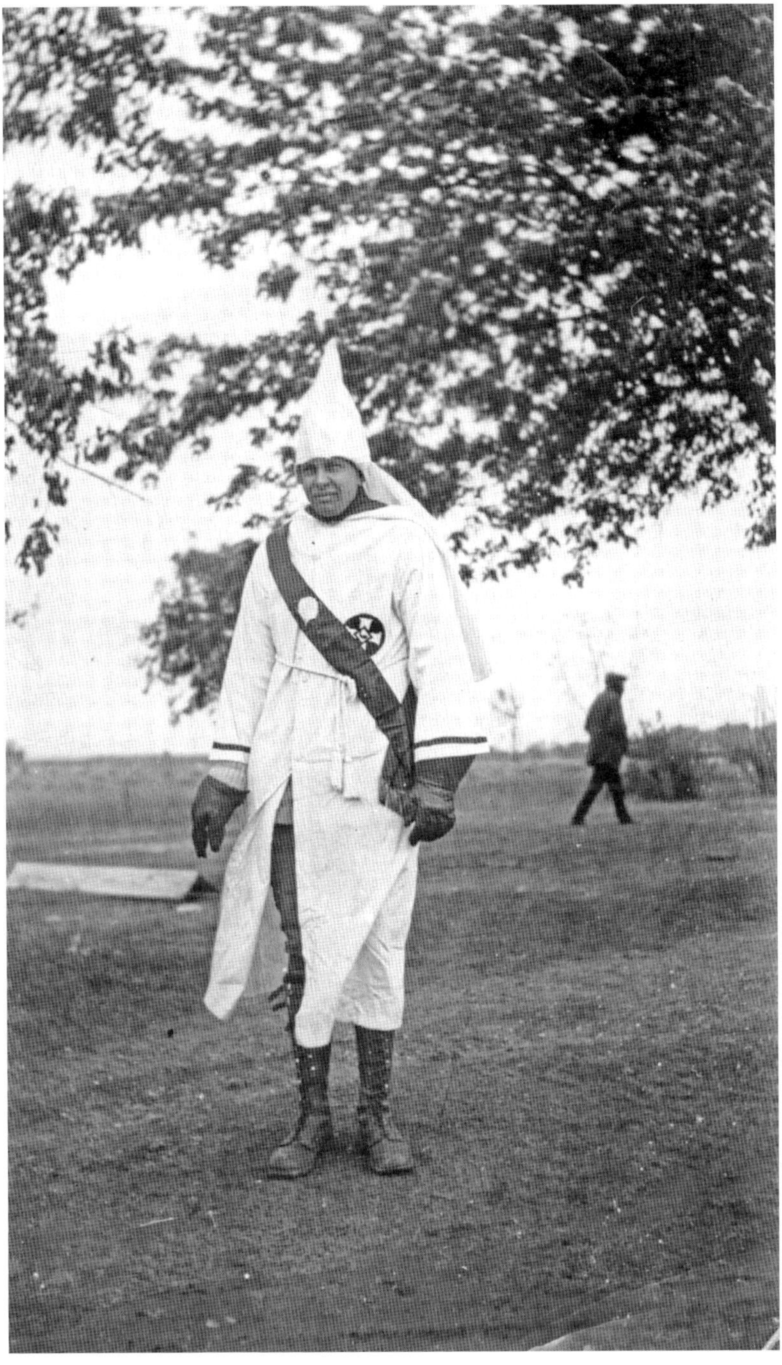

This was one of the KKK guards for the October 1925 rally in Geneva. *Geneva Historical Society.*

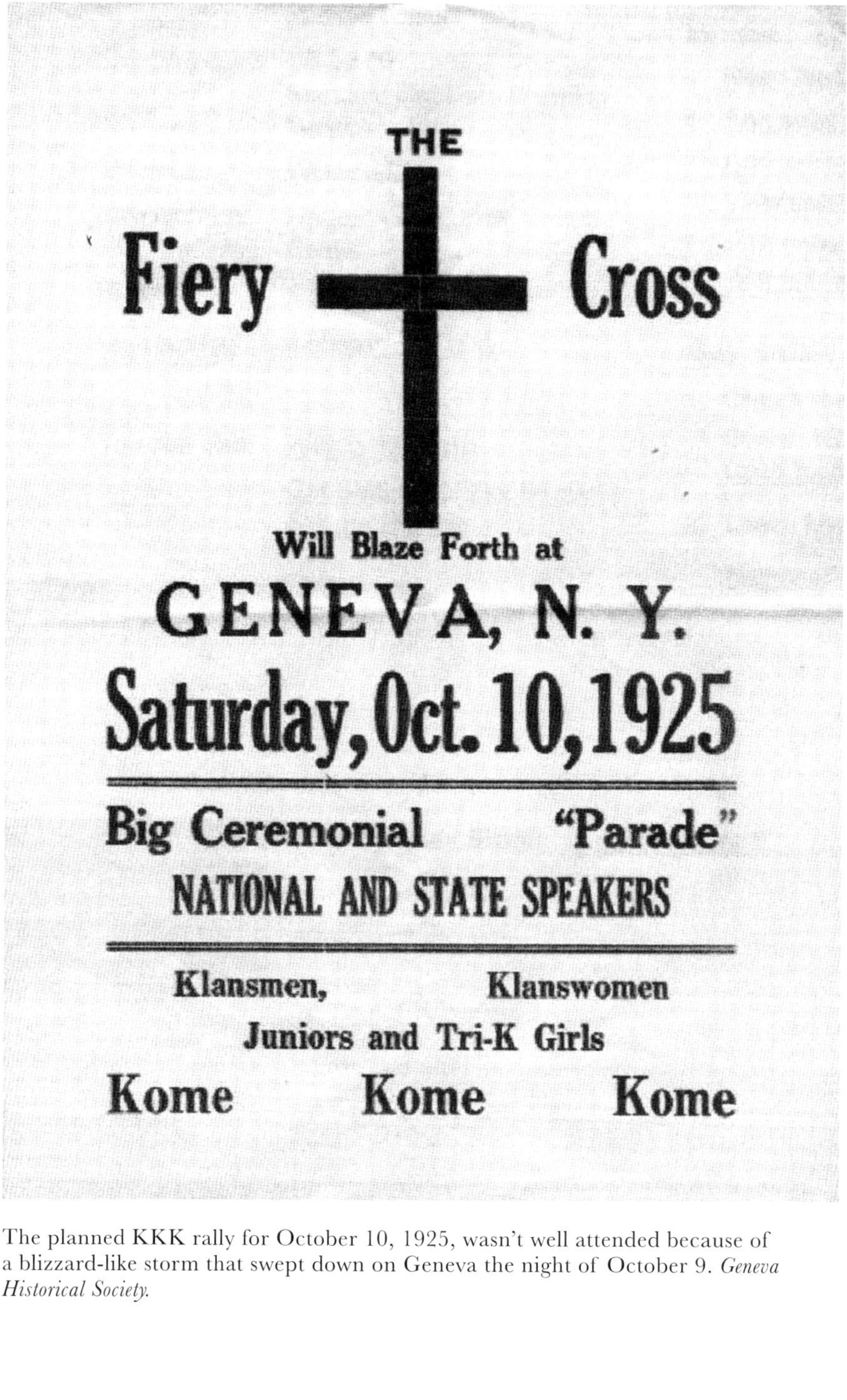
THE

Fiery Cross

Will Blaze Forth at

GENEVA, N. Y.

Saturday, Oct. 10, 1925

Big Ceremonial "Parade"

NATIONAL AND STATE SPEAKERS

Klansmen, Klanswomen

Juniors and Tri-K Girls

Kome Kome Kome

The planned KKK rally for October 10, 1925, wasn't well attended because of a blizzard-like storm that swept down on Geneva the night of October 9. *Geneva Historical Society.*

led by Sergeant Daniel Murphy of the police department, riding in a police motorcycle sidecar driven by traffic officer Spears. Traffic officer Robert Richards rode a second motorcycle. The parade went down Washington Street to Park Place and then around the park to Main Street. Moving down Seneca Street, the "long white columns [of marchers] passed between solid ranks of silent spectators. Now and then, an insult was uttered in a low voice and a few jeers sounded from the crowd. Police officers dotted the street, however, and they moved quickly to any place where trouble seemed likely to be starting." The parade group proceeded down Seneca Street, then countermarched at the Seneca Hotel and started moving back up Seneca Street. When it reached Linden Street, some trouble broke out, "the exact origin of which is not known, but it resulted in a general disturbance and the breaking of the parade ranks." What was described in the newspaper as a "street riot" took place on Seneca Street. Cordian S. Melious of Stanly was arrested, charged with wielding the club that caused a bad cut on the top of Bernard Campbell's head. Several supporters of the Klan and those opposed to it were bruised. There was also an "incident" in front of the Armory on Main Street. An aged man was knocked down, and another fight broke out, but it was quickly stopped by the police. "The parade apparently passed through Pulteney Street back to Washington Street, the starting place, without further trouble although some of the Klansmen are declared to have found the tires on their cars slashed when they returned."[133]

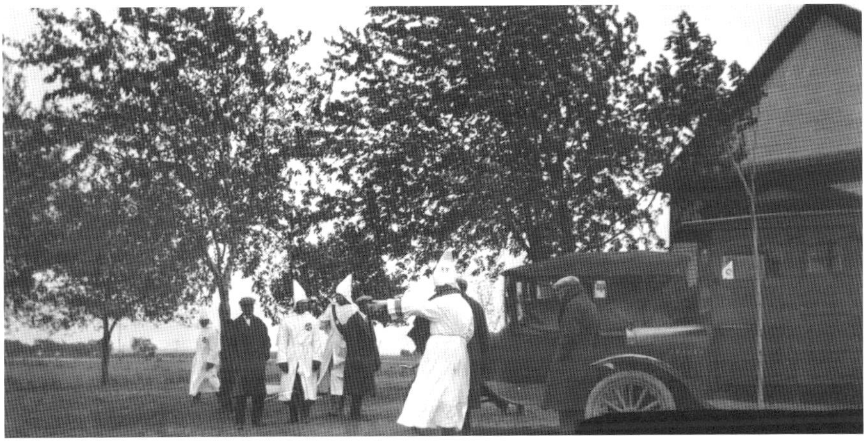

A three-day "konclave" was held at the KKK encampment near Flint, New York, in early September 1927. *Geneva Historical Society.*

Klan activity in the Geneva area was denounced by at least some local ministers. A December 1923 newspaper article told of the sermons preached by Reverend Kenneth A. Bray of St. Peter's Church. He declared the KKK organization "to be anti-Catholic, anti-racial and anti-all-things that stand for fellowship and brotherhood." He urged his parishioners to "show more fearless hostility towards the powers of darkness so suggestive of division, of separation and of hatred." He went on to say, "We honor the Christ as the Klansman's only criterion of character" that is contained in a leaflet setting forth the principles of the Klan. He went on to say that he was prejudiced, "and I thank God that I am prejudiced by one hundred and one things that the Klan apparently stands for."[134]

So, it appears safe to conclude that there was much KKK activity throughout the Finger Lakes in the 1920s, a period of great change. Some residents embraced new ways, and others sought to adhere to what they saw as traditional values.

11

The Kingdom

So The Kingdom takes its place with other lost villages of the region which Fate and Time passed by.
—*A. Glenn Rogers,* Forgotten Stories of the Finger Lakes

Although a traveler today sees virtually no physical evidence of its former existence, there was a thriving little community known as the Kingdom about midway between the Village of Waterloo and the former Village of Seneca Falls. Its location was at a small rapids that some early writings referred to as "Little Skoi-yase."[135] At one time, this village even threatened to outgrow its neighbors to the east and west. Fickle fate, however, led to its demise after a brief, but lusty, life of some forty years.[136]

Origins of the Name "Kingdom"

While the site was referred to as "Canton" on some early maps, it was better known as the "Kingdom." How it got this name is not clear. Some have claimed that it derived its name from a man named King who built a dam in the river, thus creating "King's Dam." The most widely accepted explanation is that the name the "Kingdom" came about from travelers who stopped over at this lusty, brawling sporting settlement.[137] There were at least three taverns; for many years, these establishments did not

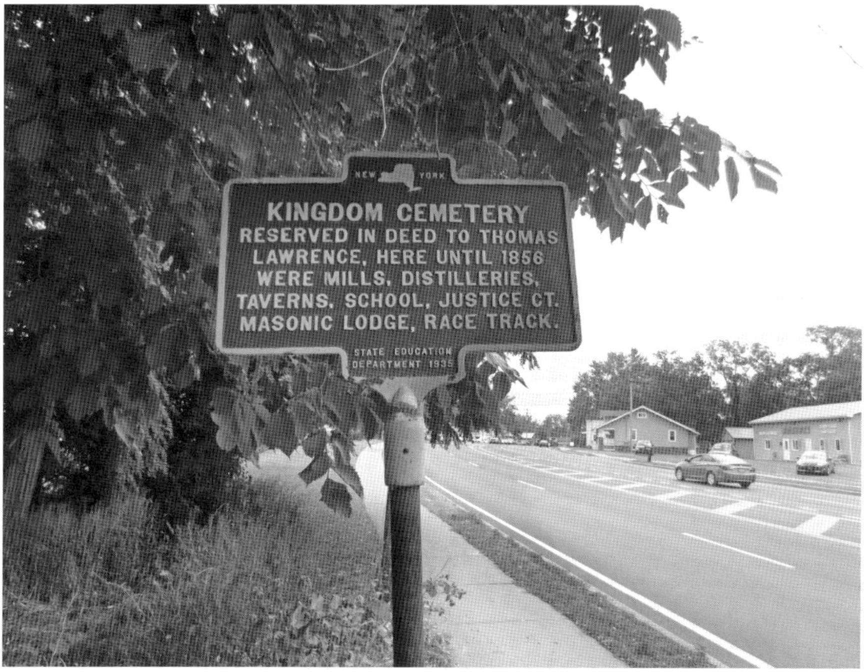

This historic marker is one of a few visible reminders of the once-thriving settlement of the Kingdom. *Walter Gable.*

have a very good reputation.[138] B.F. Beach wrote that the old natives of the area said that

> *when the distillery, stores and tavern were in a thriving condition, the day line of boats on the canal either way would head for the Kingdom and tie up for the night. The place in those days had the reputation of sporting. There were chicken and dog fights, which always resulted in fistic altercations between the native yeomanry (who styled themselves kings of the place) and the boatmen, and as the latter were outnumbered, were nearly always vanquished. Hence the name Kingdom was applied to the place.*[139]

The area might even have been named the "Devil's Kingdom," and somehow, the name was shortened to the "Kingdom."[140]

EARLY SETTLEMENT

Following the American Revolution, European American presence in the area began. Because of the Kingdom's location on the Seneca River, there was the presence of trappers and other adventurous explorers who rowed their canoes up the river.[141] Serious travel by potential settlers came with the completion of the first Cayuga Lake Bridge in 1800 and establishment of a regularly scheduled stagecoach line.

Much of the early settlement took place on the north side of the Seneca River. In 1809, Lewis Birdsall built a brick house, which he later converted to a tavern. The sand and clay used for the brick were taken from the northern portions of his property. The house was in the Colonial style, with a central entrance and wide hall. The upper story had one large room, which was used for holding court and for political purposes. In that spacious room, the first Masonic lodge in the Finger Lakes region was formed.[142] Birdsall was supervisor of the town of Junius (the Cayuga County township for all areas

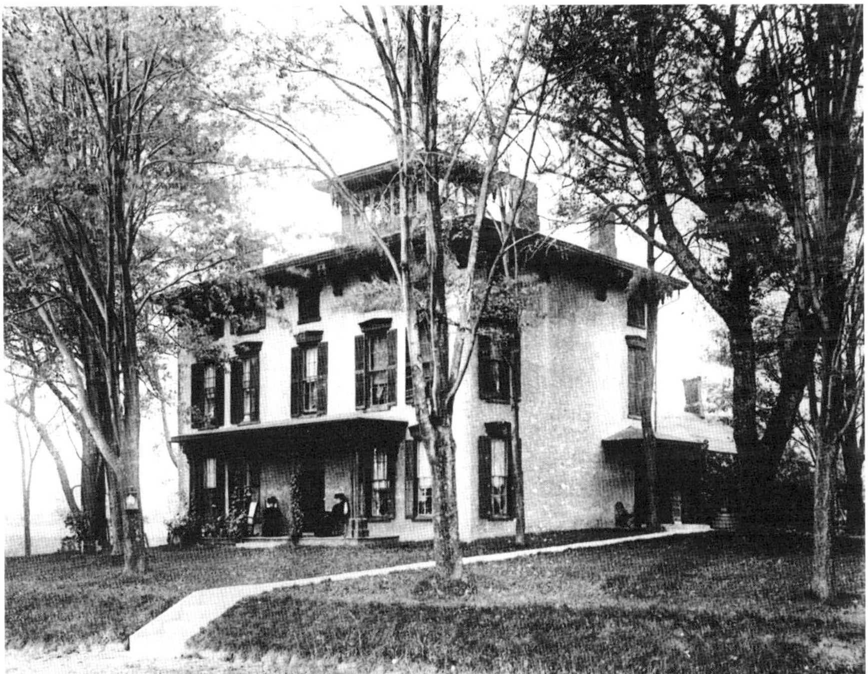

Built in 1809 by Lewis Birdsall as a home, this structure served as a tavern in the early years of the Kingdom. *Seneca County Historian's Office.*

north of the Seneca River) starting on March 1, 1803. Beginning on March 16, 1808, he served several nonconsecutive terms as county sheriff.[143]

Two other early settlers were John Knox and John Burton. Knox, the first judge of Seneca County, resigned that position to serve as a state senator from 1818 to 1820. Burton moved from Ontario County to the Kingdom in 1809. He was a volunteer in the War of 1812. After the war, he married and was a surveyor and lawyer in Waterloo. He was one of several local justices at the first general sessions of court held in the new county seat of Waterloo in 1818. From 1820 to 1822, he was a law partner with Samuel Birdsall.[144] Burton was elected a justice in 1829. His map and survey of the Village of Waterloo, made for John Sinclair & Company in 1836, became the basis of locating by lot number real estate on the north side of the river.

Another prominent resident of the Kingdom for many years was Jacob Chamberlain. He came into this area with teams of oxen, transporting heavy pieces of cannon over the Cayuga Lake Bridge during the War of 1812. Chamberlain was so pleased with the area that he purchased land in the town of Varick. In 1831, he purchased the Dimmick Farm in the Kingdom on the south side of the river. Until 1843, Jacob Chamberlain and his family lived on this farm.[145] He moved to Seneca Falls village in 1843 and became a prominent businessman and antislavery activist.

Thriving Industries

As early as 1808, there was a gristmill known as the Devereaux Mill. The water to this mill was conducted along a race that extended up the Seneca River, with a wing-dam reaching into the main channel. A history of Seneca County written in 1876 described this mill as a "rickety affair, to which motion was given by a large under-shot breast-wheel."[146]

The canal on the Seneca River created a set of locks at the Kingdom.[147] The locks led to the development of many mills on both sides of the river.[148] The locks at the Kingdom created a fall of four to five feet of water. "On the berm side a strip of land had been extended up the [Seneca] river, thus dividing the canal from the river and creating hydraulic sites and gave a stimulus to the investment of capital in manufacturing enterprises."[149] "Boats were built for freight and passengers. The packet line, far more comfortable and expeditious than the Sherwood stage, became the popular mode of travel." At the lock, Stephen Smith built a house and grocery and large barns for the accommodation of the boatmen. His son Reuben Smith built a house next to him. John Babcock put up a gristmill, plaster mill and clover mill. Adjoining these was a yard where boats were built. Deacon John Fitts, then a landlord of the tavern, with a Mr. Gilbert, erected a wool-carding and cloth factory. Matthew Sisson operated a brewery and malt house and supplied the area with beer. With all these industries, more people arrived and became residents of the Kingdom.[150]

This stimulated more economic and population growth. Hotels were enlarged. George Kuney built a half-mile racetrack, reputedly not surpassed in central New York.[151] Growth was so rapid in the Kingdom that, for a few years, it looked as if the Kingdom would surpass both Mynderse Mills (present Seneca Falls) and Skoi-yase (present Waterloo).[152] The Junius post office was located at the Kingdom, in Lewis Birdsall's store, until it was moved to Waterloo in 1816.[153] The earliest town meetings in Junius were held at the homes of various Kingdom residents between 1804 and 1821.[154] There was even talk of making the Kingdom the county seat.

The Great Western Distillery, built in 1841 on the south side of the river, east of the bridge, was the largest distillery in all of New York State. It was established by Jacob Chamberlain, Isaac Pickney, Nathaniel P. Lee and David B. Dodge. Because of its tremendous construction cost, additional financing was provided by Thomas Fatzinger, Levi Fatzinger and Joseph Wright. The large boilers were made of copper. Large pumps were used to supply the fermenting vats and for conducting the distilled spirits. The distillery was described as "the crowning business effort carrying the place, during the forties, to its height of prosperity."[155] This great distillery burned down on the night of August 5, 1846.[156] Leander Cory, who was only twelve at the time of the fire, wrote that firemen broke in the heads of many wine barrels and used them as buckets for water to put onto the fire. He added that the Waterloo Fire Department came to help fight the fire. In their haste to get a stream on the fire, one of the fire engines being backed down to the river ran off the bank. It was not pulled out of the water until the next day.[157]

AMELIA JENKS BLOOMER AND JOSEPH SMITH JR.

Interestingly, a small building near the tavern operated by George Kuney served as the school during the week and for church services on Sunday.[158] Amelia Jenks taught in this school for a term. In 1840, she married Dexter

Bloomer, and they moved to Seneca Falls. She became the publisher of the *Lily* and established herself as the first female newspaper publisher in the United States.

Another brief resident was Joseph Smith Jr., in 1823, in a small one-and-a-half-story house next to the blacksmith shop while he worked as a farmhand. A 1924 article in the *Shortsville Enterprise* said of the then-living older residents of the Kingdom area that their "impressions of him were not as a whole very flattering." This is the man who, in 1830, organized the Latter-day Saints Church at Peter Whitmer's farm in the town of Fayette.

DEMISE OF THE KINGDOM

The demise of the Kingdom came rather rapidly. A fire in 1846 destroyed the Great Western Distillery. Changes in the Cayuga-Seneca Canal eliminated the locks at the Kingdom, leaving a three-mile uninterrupted stretch of water for transportation between Seneca Falls and Waterloo. With the departure of the water power, the other mills soon disappeared. The Kingdom did not become the county seat. The advent of steam-powered trains to replace the canal packets and the stagecoach led to further population flight from the Kingdom.

Little evidence of this former thriving community has existed for years. One can still see on Routes 5 and 20, just west of Seneca Falls, the New York State historic marker for the Kingdom Cemetery. The Birdsall House, which stood nearby, is gone, removed to provide space for enlargement of the Stanton Meadows residential complex. Gone, too, is the Kingdom Bridge, which local residents used for many years as a shortcut to avoid traffic in Seneca Falls or Waterloo.

As historian A. Glenn Rogers put it, "So The Kingdom takes its place with other lost villages of the region which Fate and Time passed by."[159]

12

The Murder of John Walters and the Execution of Charles Johnson

Introduction

There are four documented executions or hangings for Seneca County murders. Indian John was hanged near Aurora on August 17, 1804, for the murder of Ezekiel Crane on December 12, 1803. (At that time, what is today Seneca County was still part of Cayuga County.)[160] John Andrews was hanged in Ovid on Friday, September 6, 1811, for the murder of an assistant with whom he worked in a distillery.[161] George Chapman was hanged in Waterloo on May 28, 1829, for the murder of Daniel Wright, with whom he had been drinking and quarreling on July 20, 1828. Reports are that between fifteen thousand and twenty thousand people crowded onto or near the island on West Water Street to see the execution.[162] On January 9, 1887, John Walters, who worked at the Seneca County Jail in Waterloo, suffered fatal blows to the head inflicted when some prisoners were trying to escape. Charles Johnson was hanged on November 15, 1888, for this death. This chapter focuses on the murder of Walters and the subsequent execution of Johnson.

Personal History of John Walters and Charles Johnson

We don't know a lot about either John Walters or Charles Johnson. Walters was described at the Johnson murder trial as being about age seventy and "rather weak and slow and clumsy. He was somewhat bent over, about 6 feet high." He was born about 1829 in the town of Fayette, New York. His father was probably James Walters. For several years, John Walters was employed as a cart man for Downs & Company at the old stone shop in Seneca Falls, located on the corner of Ovid and Green Streets. Census data for 1850 shows him living at the hotel kept by Samuel Hollenbeck in Fayette. By the time of the 1860 census, he is living in the boardinghouse of the Whitney family in Seneca Falls. He apparently is the John Walters who served in Company I of the 185th New York Infantry during the Civil War. According to 1870 census data, Walters was living with the family of Dr. Gardner Welles on the southwest corner of Oak Street in Waterloo. Prior to his becoming an employee at the jail, he had been working for Jane E. Hunt at Waterloo as a coachman.[163] He was described as a "quiet, honest, well disposed citizen."[164] Sheriff Robert Lerch said that Walters had been working at the jail for about eleven months, with the responsibilities of taking care of the barn, stoves and office and, "if I needed extra help, to furnish it."[165] He had an apartment in the jail building.[166]

Charles Johnson, twenty-seven at the time of the trial, was described as "heavily built with a rather high head." He had been held previously for minor offenses. For some time, Johnson had been living in Waterloo, where he had a married sister residing. A newspaper artist for the *Syracuse Herald* did a sketch of him at the trial.[167]

Events Leading to the Death of John Walters

The events leading up to the death of John Walters began on the night of Sunday, December 29, 1886, when two horses, equipment and other items were stolen from several places in the towns of Seneca Falls and Fayette. Edward Caldwell and Charles Johnson were arrested, charged with burglary and grand larceny and placed in the Waterloo jail. The sheriff had them shackled with an iron on each leg and eight links of chain. At mealtimes, they were let out, but at other times, they were locked in their cells. The entrance into the jail was through a wooden door in the sheriff's office and an iron-grated door. Four or five stone steps led down to the floor of the jail.[168] Johnson and Caldwell spent much of the day of January 9, 1887, removing bricks from a wall so as to escape. They began to realize that this was not going to happen soon enough, so they decided to escape by simply "rushing" the turnkey when he came in to lock them in their cells for the night.

At 7:30 p.m. on January 9, John Walters, the acting turnkey of the jail that night; John Cronin, a constable of the town of Waterloo who had come in to help during the absence of the regular turnkey; and Warren E. Lerch, the Seneca County sheriff, decided it was time to lock up the fourteen or fifteen prisoners for the night. Cronin unlocked the door, and Walters proceeded down the stone steps.[169] At the bottom, he was met by Caldwell and Johnson, who were attempting to escape.

Johnson struck Walters on the back of the head with an iron bar, and then he and Caldwell ran up the steps to attack Cronin. Cronin was struck repeatedly and fell backward against the wall, bloody and hurt. Sheriff Lerch rushed in. Lerch was a short man, apparently not strong, but he made a reputation for himself that night. He fought the two prisoners back with his club in a fierce struggle. Finally, Cronin, coming to, called out, "Shoot them, sheriff!" whereupon Lerch drew his revolver and drove the prisoners back into the jail.

Death and Funeral of John Walters

Walters was carried to his apartment in the jail building. He died there the next day as a result of the attack by Johnson and Caldwell. The *Seneca Falls Reveille* reported that Walters never regained consciousness following the attack.[170] Dr. George A. Bellows was the coroner. Soon after Walters's death on Monday afternoon, a coroner's jury was assembled, consisting of Moses Barlow, Philip Johnson, Jacob Sands, James S. Boughton, Charles Illick and J.B. Maloney. The jury rendered a verdict that John Walters came to his death by murder by Charles Johnson and Edward Caldwell, with blows inflicted by a bar or iron in the hands of Johnson and a stick of wood in the hands of Caldwell, and that it was murder in the first degree. Register no. 385 in *The Register of Deaths in the Village of Waterloo* (at the Waterloo village offices) records that John Walters died from a "compression of the brain, fracture of the skull, being hit on the head with an iron stove anvil." That record puts the time of death at 2:30 p.m. on January 10, 1887.[171] The *Auburn Bulletin* reported that the autopsy found two wounds to the head of John Walters. The first wound "was about three inches above the left eye. They also found one (wound) in the back part of the head about one and one half inches long, a y-shaped wound. The temporal bone was broken over the right ear. A fracture ran from ear to ear on the base of the skull."[172]

The *Seneca Falls Reveille* of January 14, 1887, described Walters as "the unfortunate victim of Johnson and Caldwell's murderous assault at the Waterloo jail last Sunday evening." The article described Walters as a "quiet, honest, well disposed citizen, who would not knowingly injure or molest anyone." The short article concludes with the comment, "That he should be stricken down in so brutal a manner, seems especially sad to those who have known him so long and well, and who never knew him to be guilty of a dishonorable act."[173]

The funeral of John Walters was held on January 12. A crowd of about six hundred gathered to view the body in an upstairs room in the courthouse.

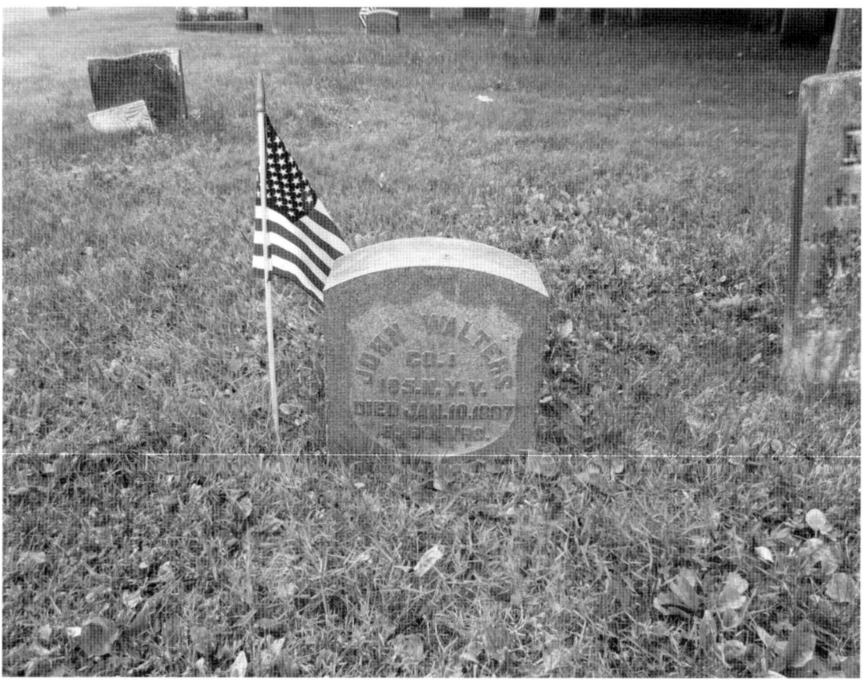

John Walters is buried in Bear Cemetery. The gravestone provides information about his Civil War service. *Walter Gable.*

The funeral itself began at 2:00 p.m., with the courtroom, halls and offices "nearly filled while another large congregation was on the sidewalk about the jail and across the road in the park, it being impossible to obtain admission to the court house." Reverend Monger of the Methodist Episcopal Church conducted the services. He took for his text the words, "Where is thy life?" He spoke feelingly of the victim's fate. Reverend White of the Presbyterian Church pronounced the benediction. Walters's remains were encased in a black, cloth-covered coffin with silver mountings. Members of the local Grand Army of the Republic (GAR) Snyder Post attended in a body and acted as bearers of the body. "A large number of carriages composed the cortege while over three hundred walked to the grave yard to witness the burial." The burial took place in the Bear Cemetery.[174]

Trial and Execution of Charles Johnson

The trial of Charles Johnson began on April 4, 1887, before Judge Francis A. Macomber. The prosecuting attorneys were District Attorney Francis Allen of Ovid and his assistant, Colonel F.L. Manning of Waterloo. The defending attorneys were Corydon Rood and the Honorable William H. Burton assisting. The men were tried separately. The jury in the Johnson trial consisted of Henry Jinks (a Waterloo farmer), Spencer Hoffman (a Junius farmer), Nelson Seekel (a Tyre farmer), Spencer White (a Tyre farmer), Charles Whitlock (a Seneca Falls farmer), Columbus Christopher (a traveling man), George Troutman (a Fayette farmer), Henry S. Bonnell (a Waterloo farmer), Patrick J. Maloney (a Waterloo farmer), Edward Bear (a Junius farmer) and George W. Barlow (a Tyre farmer). Being the first murder trial in this county for more than half a century, the event naturally drew great interest. One newspaper described the throngs seeking to attend at least part of the trial this way: "A terrible crowd demanded admission at 2 p.m., hundreds more than could be accommodated and hundreds more were turned away."[175] The *Syracuse Weekly Express* described the trial as follows:

> *Sheriff Lerch testified to receiving the prisoner and having him in custody, from commitment by Justice Guion. Richard Stone, of Chicago, who was in the jail as a vagrant at the time of the assault, testified on the movements of the prisoners inside the jail. He testified that Fisk sawed Johnson's shackles off with a notched cane knife. The knives and shackles were shown*

to the jury. The prisoners dug into the jail wall. Witness carried away the bricks. Mrs. Kelly visited the jail to pray for prisoners. After she left the jail Caldwell secured a club and asked if it was heavy enough to hit a man with. A jail diagram was shown to witness, who further said that the prisoners assembled in Caldwell's cell. Caldwell said that he would fight his way out. When witness heard the doors open he ran toward the water closet so as not to see the affray. When he came back John Walters was lying at the foot of the stone steps.

On cross examination he said that Johnson threatened to slug the sheriff. Witness told them not to hurt old John, the man that was killed, and Johnson replied, you will not be to blame if we do. On turning back from the water closet, he saw Fisk holding the iron door and yelling "get there! Get there." Then he heard the sheriff order them to "get back" and he saw Caldwell and Johnson run back to their cells.

Another prisoner, George Flaherty, who was committed in December for disorderly conduct testified that he heard the filing of shackles in Fisk's cell. When the affray occurred he stood with his back toward the steps. Saw Fisk pull the iron door open. He caught John Walters by the leg. Next saw Walters lying on the floor. Heard running up and down the steps. Saw the sheriff on the steps with revolvers, and heard him threaten to shoot any man that moved. He called help to pick up Walters. He saw blood near Walters' head. I helped carry him to the office. I heard him moan.

Justice Guion testified as to the commitment for theft; then another prisoner, John Kissinger, testified as follows: I was in my jail bed from after dinner till Mrs. Kelly, jail missionary, came. Heard something fall like a soft body. Heard Fisk crying "get there." Saw Walters lying on the floor in about a quart of blood. Was made sick at sight and went back to my cell. Heard noise of fighting and heard Walters moan. The sheriff and Cronin came in at that and locked up the man and searched the jail.

Sheriff Lerch being recalled testified: I visited Romulus that Sunday. Left Cronin in charge of the jail. Employed Walters to take care of barn, office and store. Cronin handed keys to Walters who went down late [to the] *jail. Heard front door close and Cronin yell three times, "Sheriff, get your club, they're coming!" Saw Cronin back out of door and stagger, with his hands up. Jumped in between him and prisoners. Saw Johnson with stove shaker and Caldwell with stick two and a half feet long. Johnson was ahead. Saw Johnson and was struck by him with the iron. My wound was one and one-fourth inches in length, on the head. Kept striking with my club twenty or twenty-five times at Johnson. Saw Caldwell strike over*

> *John's shoulder. Caldwell was advancing, Cronin cried "Sheriff, pull your revolver." I stopped to pull my revolver which caught momentarily in my pocket. Johnson threw the iron, struck my hat and knocked it off. Johnson then ran back. Followed prisoners to doors. Saw them running from west to north corridor. I turned back and told Cronin to fetch a policeman, McCue. I went down into the jail. Saw Walters lying on his back, moaning, with a pool of blood under his head. I lifted him partially by the waist. I said to a couple of prisoners, "Come here and take this man up." They assisted and carried him into the office. I went out and examined outside of jail to see if there was any hole in the wall. I saw citizens congregating in the court house and told Officer McCue to get men and search the jail. Caldwell, Johnson and Fisk were found in their cells and McCue found the knives. Walters died at 11 o'clock on Monday afternoon and was buried Wednesday. My daughter picked up the iron thrown by Johnson.*
>
> *Officer Cronin then testified to Mrs. Kelley's visit, and then added in record to the affray: "I saw Charles Johnson strike John Walters with the stove shaker, and also saw Edward Caldwell strike Walters with the stick. Johnson rushed up the steps and struck me with the iron. (Witness exhibited marks on his hand where the scar appeared.) I put up my hands to ward away the blows. Caldwell struck at me. The stick was too long and caught at top of door. I saw Johnson throw the shaker at Sheriff Lerch. I went down Main Street blowing my signal whistle to summon Officer McCue."*
>
> *Wm. H. Burton, Esq., summed up for the prisoner and Col. F.L. Manning for the people. The charge of Judge Macomber was clear, concise, and impartial. The jury went out at 4 o'clock and after having come in to inquire of the judge in regard to some point of law, rendered their verdict at 8:00 as stated above, murder in the first degree.*[176]

The *Seneca County Courier* summed up the trial this way: "The austerity of the trial is unusual. But the case was very simple so far as the range of testimony was concerned, and the district attorney and his assistant had carefully guarded against technical difficulties. The defendant's counsel did all that could be done for a client so circumstanced, and the universal judgment of the community is that the verdict is a righteous one."[177]

The trial of Caldwell began on April 11, 1887, with the same attorneys as for the Johnson trial. The verdict in this case was murder in the second degree.

It developed during the trial that one Marcus Fisk, a prisoner in the jail at the time, had sawed off the shackles of Johnson and Caldwell with a saw made from a table knife and had attempted to dig a hole through the brick walls of the jail so as to escape. Not being able to make a hole large enough, they had determined to go through the door when the turnkey came in to close up for the night.

Johnson was sentenced to hang on May 25, but his case was appealed. He was re-sentenced to hang on November 15, 1888. Caldwell was given life imprisonment, and Fisk was convicted of manslaughter and sent to the Elmira Reformatory.

Johnson was hanged on a scaffold erected in the jail. These gallows were brought in from Utica, where they had been used for two previous executions. The gallows were in the jail corridor; the south windows were darkened with canvas. Forty guards were placed outside the jail, twenty from Cross Post and twenty from Tyler J. Snyder Post, GAR. A few members of the press were admitted. All this reflected Sheriff Lerch's determination to take every precaution "to attain the privacy which the law enjoins."[178] Lerch read the death warrant to Johnson at 8:40 a.m. At 10:15 a.m., the sheriff led the way to the scaffold, followed by Johnson and Reverend W.S. Carter. The execution took place at 10:22 a.m.

Some Concluding Comments

The events leading to the death of John Walters apparently prompted action to be taken to improve conditions at the Seneca County Jail. The January 14, 1887 issue of the *Seneca Falls Reveille* reported that "it is gratifying to know the supervisors are to meet at Waterloo today to take necessary steps toward rendering the jail at that place more secure than it is now. This should have been done long ago. Persons have no difficulty, if they were so disposed, in escaping from its walls. It has been a constant menace to the officers charged with its care and protection. It is neither a safe place to be guarded by the officers of the law. The terrible event of last Sunday night was not needed to demonstrate its insecurity and danger."[179] The January 21, 1887 issue reported that the board of supervisors had met in special session and approved $600 "to put the jail in safe and proper condition. The present jail is not an old one and the expenditure was judicious."[180]

On October 10, 2009, the Seneca County Sheriff's Office dedicated a permanent memorial to Walters on the grounds of the Seneca County Law

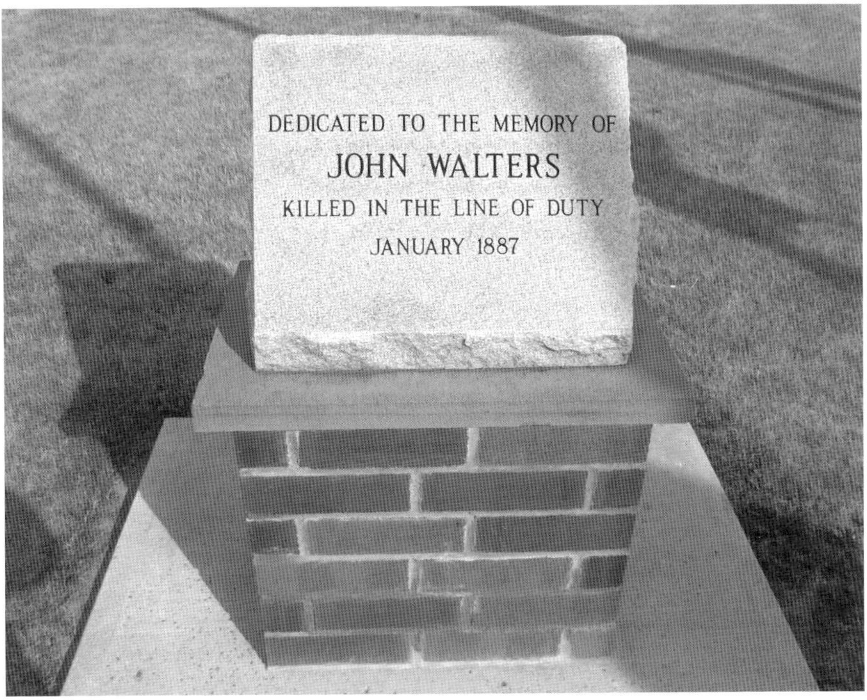

On October 10, 2009, the Seneca County Law Enforcement Center memorial to John Walters was dedicated. He is the only county law enforcement staff member to be killed while on duty. *Walter Gable.*

Enforcement Center and dedicated the training room as the John Walters Memorial Training Room. Undersheriff Gary Sullivan pointed out, "As we conduct training of our deputies and others, his story is a reminder of the dangerous work we do. It was an honor for all of us who worked on this project to ensure John Walters' sacrifice is not forgotten."[181]

That same year, the Seneca County Sheriff's Department successfully nominated John Walters for inclusion at the National Law Enforcement Officers Memorial in Washington, D.C. It is located in the 400 block of E Street. Its blue-gray marble walls are inscribed with the names of more than 17,500 officers who have been killed in the line of duty. Each May, during National Police Week, new names of fallen officers are added.

When the Seneca County historian visited the memorial in March 2015, he brought back a rubbing of Walters's name inscribed on that panel, as well as a memorial banner. Those items have been added to the display on the wall of the John Walters Memorial Training Room.

It is good that the Seneca County Sheriff's Department has chosen to honor John Walters, who, over 120 years ago, lost his life in service to the county. Given the state-of-the-art facility we have today, it is somewhat difficult to appreciate the deplorable conditions of the Seneca County Jail at the time of Walters's death.

A total of 1,130 individuals have been executed (after being given the death penalty) in New York State. The last execution was of Eddie Lee Mays on August 15, 1963. In 1965, New York State eliminated the death penalty for most crimes. In July 1972, the U.S. Supreme Court invalidated all existing death penalty laws. From 1974 to 1978, attempts to reinstate the death penalty were struck down by the courts. From 1978 to 1994, death penalty legislation routinely passed the state legislature but was vetoed by Governors Hugh Carey and Mario Cuomo. Following through on his campaign pledge, Governor George Pataki, in September 1995, signed a law reinstating the death penalty and a life-without-parole sentencing option. In June 2004, the state's court of appeals ruled that this new law was unconstitutional.[182] So, if an incident similar to the death of John Walters were to happen today to a jail employee or law officer, the person found guilty of such a murder could not be given the death penalty.

While John Walters was a rather common man, one cannot overlook the fact that he lost his life because of injuries inflicted while he was working as a Seneca County employee. The honors extended to John Walters are justly deserved. In the spring of 2015, Undersheriff Gary Sullivan said, "The story of his [Walters's] service to the citizens of Seneca County should not go untold and his memory should not be forgotten."[183]

13
Degory Prowtt

Along Route 89, just south of Swick Road, there is a historic marker for Degory Prowtt, who served as a drummer boy in the American Revolution. His name is spelled in different ways in the records—Prowtt, Proutt, Prout, Prouth. For consistency, this chapter uses the spelling that appears on the historic marker.

Degory Prowtt was born on May 13, 1761, in Cornwall, on the Surrey side of London. His father, Thomas Prout, was an Irish sea captain. His mother was Charity Hawke, the niece of Edward Hawke, the Baron of Towton and the First Lord of the Admiralty. Thomas and Charity had three sons, the youngest of whom was Degory. In 1763, Thomas and Charity and their three sons moved to New York, where Thomas continued as a sea captain. Unfortunately, on a third trip to India, Thomas and his two eldest sons were lost at sea.

When Degory was about thirteen, his mother apprenticed him to a trade. Feeling ill treated, Degory ran away and enlisted as a drummer boy under Captain James Greig on March 4, 1776, in the Third New York Continental Regiment, commanded by Colonel Peter Gansevoort. He was later transferred to Captain Jacob Rutsen DeWitt's company and then to Captain John Van Sitze's in the same regiment. In 1780, the latter company was transferred to the First New York Regiment, commanded by Colonel G. Van Schaick.

Prowtt was present at the siege of Fort Stanwix in August 1777. Colonel Gansevoort had refused British brigadier general Barry St. Leger's terms of surrender of the fort (which was now renamed Fort Schuyler). Gansevoort's

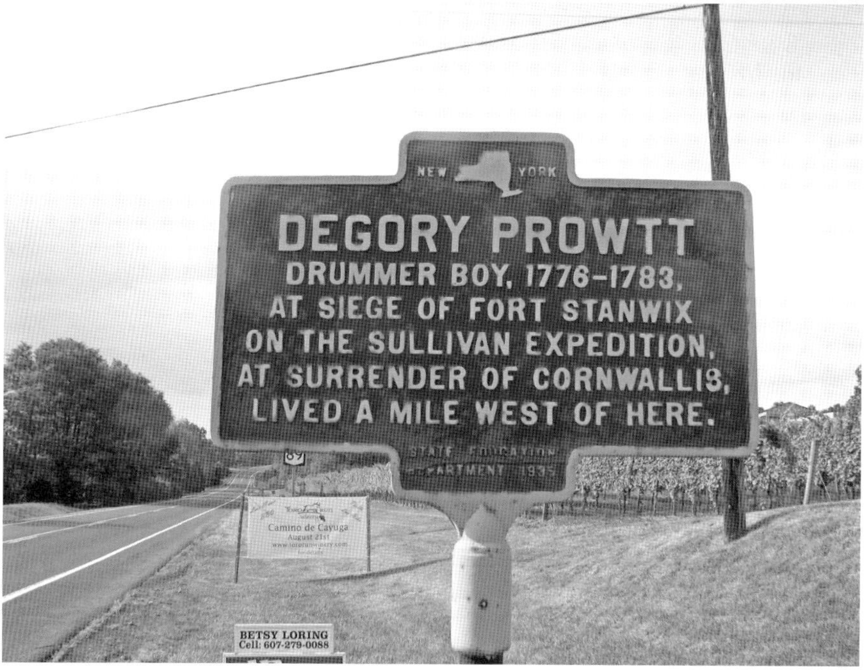

Degory Prowtt was a drummer boy during the Revolutionary War and then lived most of the rest of his life in the town of Romulus. *Walter Gable.*

soldiers held out valiantly for twenty days until reinforcements under Benedict Arnold arrived, forcing St. Leger's British forces to withdraw. The failure of the British to capture this fort helps to explain why the British did not gain control of the Mohawk Valley during the Revolutionary War. In 1778 and 1779, Prowtt was part of detachments on duty at several points in the Mohawk Valley and Albany. Prowtt took part in the so-called Sullivan Expedition against the Iroquois Indians in 1779. This means that Prowtt was on lands that would become Seneca County. Following the Sullivan Expedition, his regiment spent the winter at Morristown, New Jersey. It was then posted in the Highlands of the Hudson River for much of the remainder of the war.

The Prowtt family has a wonderful story about the quick-thinking actions of Degory in an incident during General Sullivan's campaign against the Iroquois. As the story goes, Degory was crossing a bridge when he spied a crouching Indian. Degory quickly aimed his drumstick at the Indian's head and dealt so powerful a blow that it killed the Indian. The family story goes on to say that Degory used the tanned skin from the Indian's back for his drumhead.

Prowtt also served at the Battle of Yorktown, the last real conflict of the Revolution. It must have been quite an experience for Prowtt to witness the surrender of General Charles Cornwallis on October 17, 1781!

During the Revolutionary War, Degory's mother, Charity, had tried to reconcile with her family, an estrangement that arose because of their opposition to her marrying Thomas Prout. Charity's brother, a merchant in London, named her and her sons as his heirs. Charity decided to wait until Degory returned from the war before she would go back to England and reconcile with her brother. Unfortunately, just a few days after Degory returned, Charity died of yellow fever. Degory decided to try to make a success of himself in America before going to England and claiming the inheritance that would eventually come from his uncle.

Prowtt married twice. About 1784, he married Jemima Sherwood of Massachusetts. They had four children: William, Daniel, Thomas and Jemima.

A few years after his first marriage, Prowtt learned of his uncle's death. On two different occasions, his wife's family scuttled his plans to go to London to claim his uncle's inheritance. About 1825, Prowtt entrusted a Methodist minister named John B. Youngs to take his paperwork for his claim when Youngs went to London. All traces of the minister and Prowtt's paperwork were lost.

In recognition of his services in the army, New York gave Prowtt six hundred acres in the township of Solon, in what is now Cortland County. As so many Revolutionary War soldiers did, Prowtt sold and deeded away these lands. In Prowtt's case, he turned over his property—which was then a wilderness—to Stephen Hogeboom of Claverick for fifteen pounds. According to a history of the town of Romulus, Degory Prowtt settled on Lot 84 in Romulus. It is easy to speculate that he, like other soldiers in the Sullivan Expedition, such as Lawrence Van Cleef, saw the natural beauty and economic potential of the lands they traversed while destroying Iroquois settlements and decided to settle in this area. According to the December 13, 1834 Romulus assessment roll, Prowtt owned eight acres on Lot 84, worth ninety-six dollars for a tax levy of twenty-six cents! He had purchased this property from Asa and Catharine Church on September 27, 1820. Family records report that Prowtt was so bothered by arthritis that only four acres of his property had been "cleared" for farming.

While a resident of Seneca County, on May 4, 1818, he applied for a veteran's pension. He received eight dollars a month. The history of the

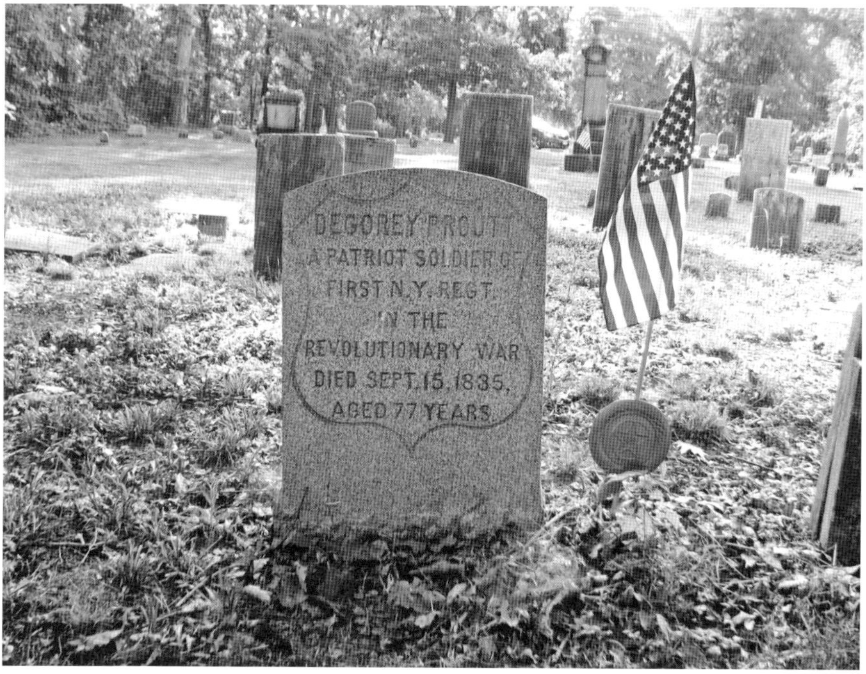

Degory Prowtt is buried in the Oak Hill Cemetery in McDuffietown. *Walter Gable.*

town of Romulus stated that he was a local Methodist exhorter (preacher). He was a member of the First Methodist Church of Varick at McDuffietown.

His wife, Jemima, died on February 26, 1833. In 1835, Prowtt married Hannah Ball, a widow with two daughters. He lived just a few months after this second marriage. On September 15, 1835, he summoned his neighbors Aaron and Titus Phillips to be witnesses to a will he had made out. He bequeathed his land, two cows, household goods, the family Bible, his watch, a big clock and books to various heirs. He died on September 20 at age seventy-seven and was buried in the Oak Hill Cemetery at McDuffietown. His widow, Hannah, died in 1847 and was buried next to Prowtt.

Visiting Prowtt's grave today, one has only some sense of his exciting experiences during the Revolutionary War. Approximately one hundred Revolutionary War veterans are buried in Seneca County. The local chapter of the Sons of the American Revolution has been actively seeking to attain information about each of these soldiers and, if necessary, to errect new gravestones justly honoring the war sacrifices of these individuals.[184]

14

The Three Bears in Ovid

The half-shire public buildings of Seneca County, pleasantly situated on a knoll fronting Courthouse Square in the Village of Ovid—now commonly called the "Three Bears"—are among the best-known historical landmarks in the scenic Finger Lakes region. The largest of the brick buildings, the courthouse, is affectionately called "Papa Bear." Next, to the south (the middle of the three buildings), is the "Mama Bear." Then comes the smallest of the three—the "Baby Bear." The Historic Preservation League of New York State indicates that these structures are unique in the

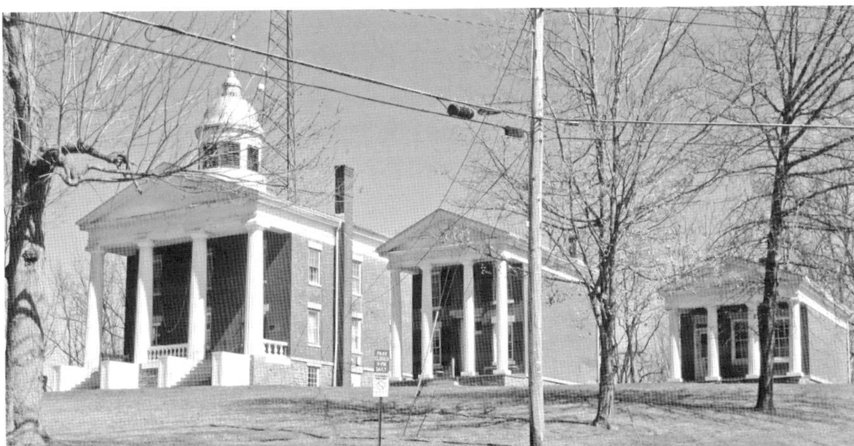

The Three Bears complex in Ovid is the only set in the entire United States of three adjacent, intact Greek Revival public buildings. *Walter Gable.*

entire United States—there is no other intact set of three adjacent public buildings of the Greek Revival style of architecture. That helps to explain why they are listed in the National Register of Historic Places.

The courthouse was erected in 1845 as a replacement for the original wooden courthouse building, which had deteriorated and become unsafe. The building contract was awarded to the brothers Obadiah B. Latham Jr. and Oliver S. Latham of Seneca Falls. Obadiah was an architect and civil engineer. As was typical for nineteenth-century courthouse construction in New York, architects and builders were chosen for demonstrated competence, and their work was carefully supervised by an appointed committee. For this construction project, the committee consisted of Elijah Denton, Dr. Claudius C. Coan and Clement Jones. Clement Jones and Sidney Grant drew up the plans for the courthouse. Bricks for the courthouse and the clerk's office (the Baby Bear) were produced locally at John B. Seeley's farm. The use of local materials not only kept costs down but also served to benefit suppliers and builders in the area.

The new courthouse (Papa Bear) and the clerk's office (Baby Bear) were impressive Greek Revival brick structures with Doric porticos. The cupola

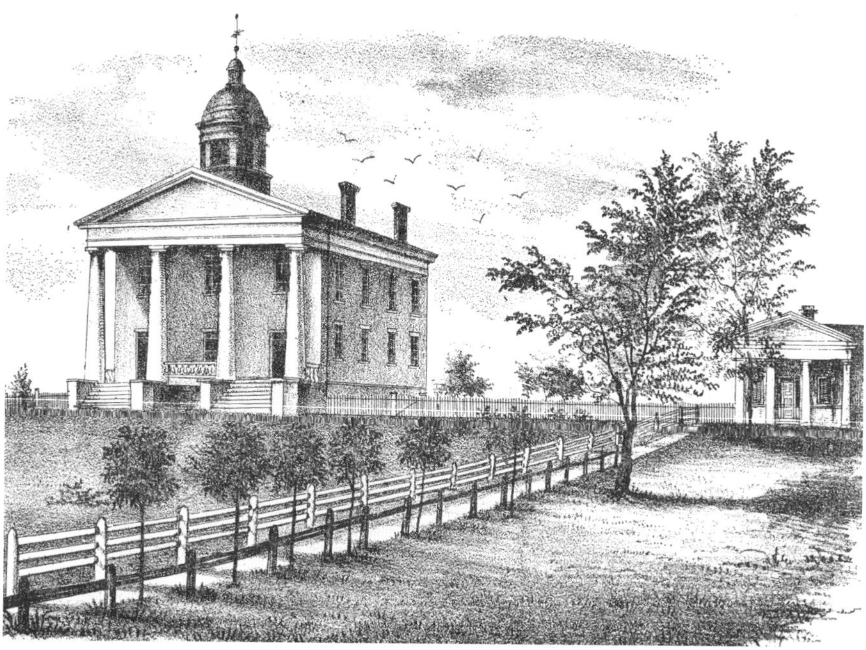

A drawing shows the Papa Bear and the Baby Bear buildings before construction of the Mama Bear structure. *Ovid Historical Society.*

of the courthouse was crowned with a weathervane reportedly from the first courthouse. The basement of the courthouse housed a kitchen, dining room and stone jail with three cells. Two of these cells have doors of riveted iron bars secured with padlocks. The third cell has a solid steel-plate door with a single opening—the only source of light or fresh air. The sheriff's living quarters and office were housed on the first floor so that he was available on-site at all hours. The grand jury room was also located on the first floor. The large courtroom with its tall ceiling and windows and tiered seating is located on the second floor. Like its predecessor, the new courthouse was the setting not only for trials and political debate but also for concerts, lectures and meetings of community organizations. One of the most celebrated speakers to give a lecture in the courthouse was Horace Greeley, editor of the *New York Tribune*, who spoke there on September 30, 1857.[185]

The design of the first clerk's office (Baby Bear), with its Doric temple front, was similar to that of the courthouse, though on a smaller scale. The flooring of the loft was fireproof, with a thick layer of ash to help protect the county's records. The records, stoves and furniture of the two county clerk's offices (Ovid and Waterloo) were moved from one to the other at the close of each three-year term. Ten teams of horses were required for transporting the equipment and records. The Committee on County Buildings rented out the clerk's office at Ovid during those terms when the clerk was in Waterloo. This arrangement continued until about 1905, when the clerk's office remained permanently in Waterloo.

In its early days, Courthouse Square was rented out to farmers as a pasture for cattle and hogs, but in the years following the completion of the new courthouse in 1845, the square was regraded and reseeded, trees were planted and fencing was installed around its perimeter. Stone walks were installed in the square beginning in 1869.

In 1859, it was decided that a new clerk's office was needed. Local builder Horace H. Bennett and mason Tunis S. Van Horn were contracted to build it on the site between the courthouse and the old clerk's office. Work began in

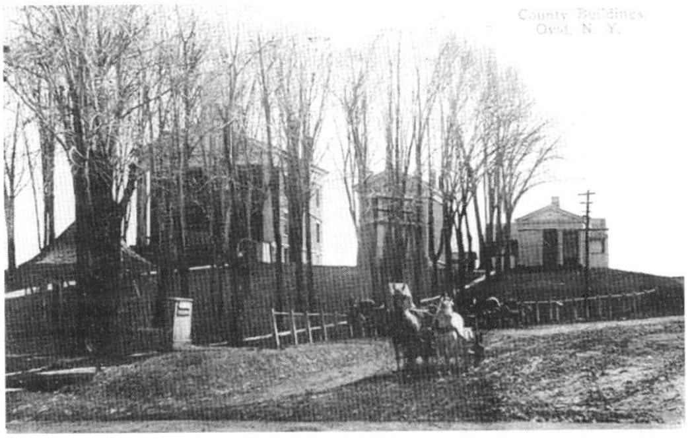

A circa 1900 postcard view shows the Three Bears buildings atop a village park on a hill. *Seneca County Historian's Office.*

1860 and was completed in 1862. The Greek Revival temple-front design of the clerk's office (Mama Bear) complemented the design of the two older buildings at the complex.

The Three Bears have been used for various purposes throughout the years. The Papa Bear ceased to be the site of court sessions sometime before 1975. This was largely because the courtroom is not accessible to the disabled. The Seneca County Board of Supervisors occasionally meets in the Ovid courtroom. Following the resignation of Undersheriff Gerald Brewer in 1974, the jail and undersheriff's quarters were no longer used in that capacity. The Papa Bear today still contains a satellite office of the Office for the Aging.

Mama Bear served as the county clerk's office, alternating terms with the Waterloo office, from its completion in 1862 until 1905, when it became the Ovid Free Library. The building served in this capacity until 1962, when it became the health center of the Seneca County Department of Health. In 1974, when the health department moved into Papa Bear, Mama Bear became a satellite office for the Seneca County Sheriff's Department. It continues in this capacity today.

After the completion of a new county clerk's office (Mama Bear) in 1862, the old clerk's office (Baby Bear) became the county surrogate's office for alternating terms. Baby Bear was also once used as a temporary facility for a local bank after a disastrous fire destroyed most of the business portion of the village on October 13, 1874. Sometime later, the Baby Bear was used almost exclusively by the Grand Army of the Republic, the organization of Union veterans of the Civil War. As these veterans passed away, the Sons of Union Veterans, Caywood Chapter, the successor organization of the local chapter of the GAR, has continued to use the Baby Bear exclusively.

The Three Bears are outstanding local interpretations of the nationally popular Greek Revival style. This was the dominant style of American architecture from the 1830s to the 1850s, used for houses, schools, churches, commercial buildings, courthouses and other government buildings. The style's popularity in this country was partly due to its symbolic association with the democratic ideals of ancient Greece. The style was widely disseminated by carpenters' pattern books, including Asher Benjamin's *The Practical House Carpenter* and *The American Builder's Companion*. Mama Bear, completed in 1862, is a relatively late example of the style and has more attenuated proportions, but it was compatible in design with the existing buildings.[186]

Many of the historic county courthouses in New York State were built in the Greek Revival style. The symmetry, dignity and formality of this style reflected the high regard in which law and local government were held. The Papa Bear courthouse is architecturally significant as an example of an intact mid-1800s courtroom. It possesses a high level of period architectural integrity and retains many of its original materials and features. Typical of nineteenth-century courtroom architecture, the Ovid courtroom is graced with large windows (on three walls) and a tall ceiling. The judge's bench, jury boxes and witness chair were placed on elevated platforms so they could be seen clearly from anywhere in the room. The seating in the courtroom was tiered and curved to allow for better viewing by the public.

In recent years, Seneca County government has been moving away from using the Three Bears. Fortunately, a group known as the Friends of the Three Bears has emerged to spearhead efforts to maintain the buildings and to put them to use to enhance tourism, promotion of local history and other beneficial economic uses. On November 20, 2003, the Preservation League of New York State designated the Three Bears as one of New York State's "Seven to Save," the nonprofit group's annual list of the state's most threatened historic places. Thanks to the efforts of the Friends of the Three Bears, extensive renovation has taken place to the Mama Bear and Papa Bear. Work is beginning on renovation of the Baby Bear, which is leased to the Caywood Camp, Sons of Union Veterans.

15

The Waterloo Organ Company

For many years, a thriving business in Waterloo was producing well-built organs and pianos that were sold throughout the United States. In its years of operation, the company changed its name several times.

The manufacture of Waterloo Cabinet Organs began in 1861, with a very small plant that developed into one of the largest and best-equipped organ factories in the United States. It is still possible to purchase a Waterloo Pump Organ on eBay or Craigslist.

A disastrous fire on May 27, 1881, destroyed the manufacturing plant on the east side of Virginia Street.[187] Then, Alexander C. Reed and Malcolm Love, his nephew, purchased the Waterloo Organ Manufacturing Company and renamed it Malcolm Love and Company. In 1888, the firm was incorporated as the Waterloo Organ Company, with Reed serving as president.[188]

The Waterloo Organ Company decided in 1889 to manufacture pianos as well as organs. It engaged a skilled piano builder by the name of Seebald Mennig, who drew up the scale (the interior plan of the piano, including the length of the strings and the method of putting in the sounding board) for Malcolm Love Piano. Benjamin B. Knight purchased the first piano that was manufactured. Knight's son William D. Knight later donated this piano to the Waterloo Library and Historical Society; it is still on display in its Terwilliger Museum.[189]

Opposite, bottom: This Waterloo Organ Company building was located on Washington Street. *Waterloo Library and Historical Society.*

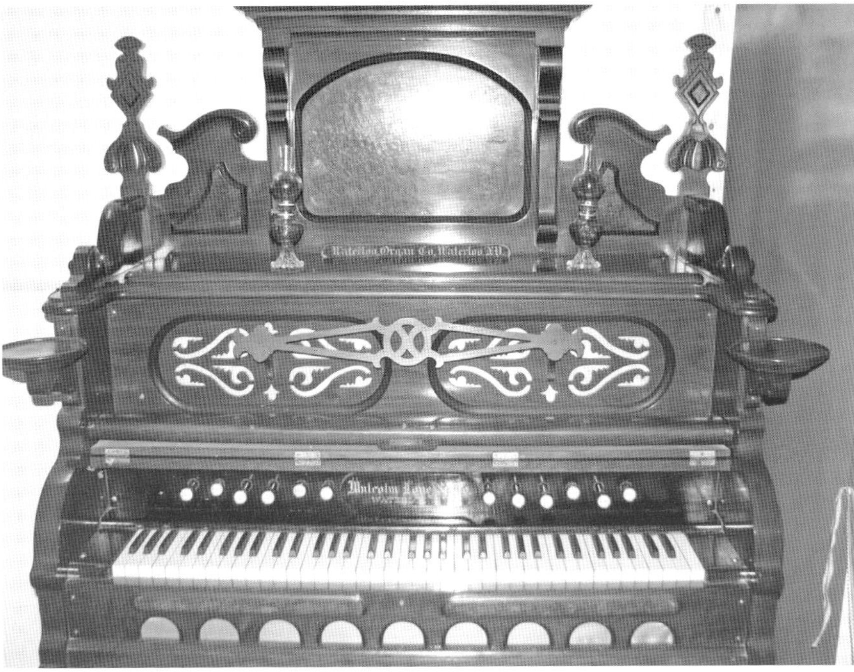

Reed organs, like this Malcom Love and Company model, became a familiar sight in the parlors of many homes in the late 1800s and early 1900s. *Waterloo Library and Historical Society.*

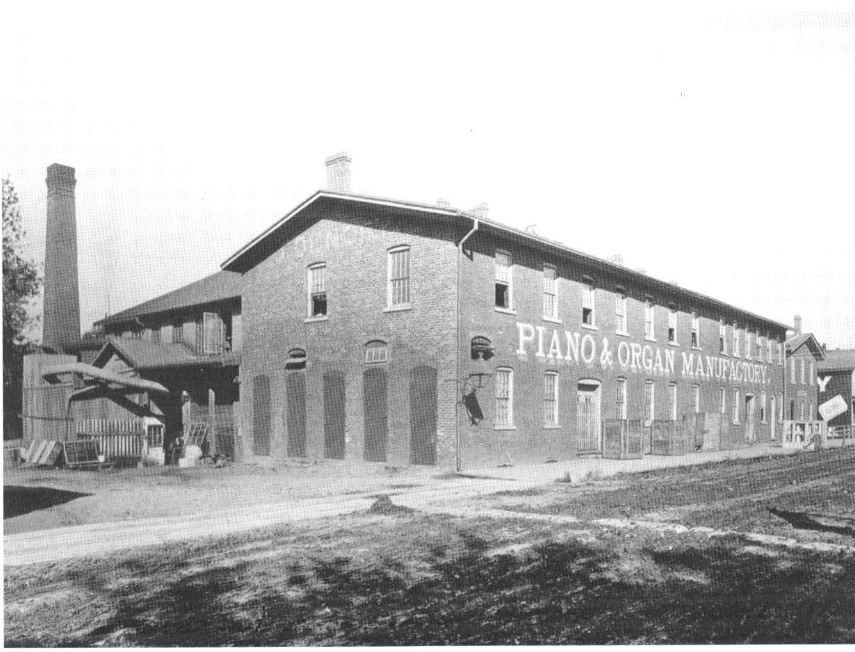

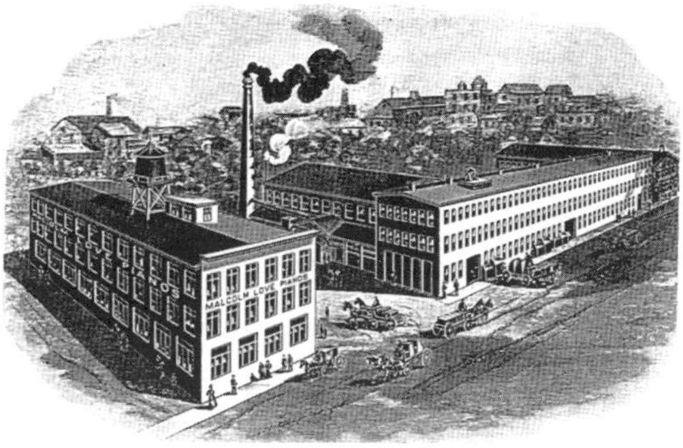

Malcolm Love Pianos were made in these buildings. *Waterloo Library and Historical Society.*

At the World's Columbian Exposition in Chicago in 1893, the Waterloo Organ Company had a booth where it displayed its Malcolm Love Piano. This piano received an award for its fine quality of tone and good workmanship, equal to the award of any piano exhibited. An official ribbon was awarded, a copy of which was attached to the back of each Malcolm Love Piano as long as they were thereafter manufactured in Waterloo. The company also received a bronze medal.[190]

Tragedy struck on Saturday evening, March 13, 1897, when the piano-finishing factory burned. This was the old Waterloo Yeast Company building, rented by the Waterloo Organ Company from Adolf Semtner. It was located on the east side of Church Street, the second door north of Main Street. The patterns, tools and machinery of the piano company were destroyed at a loss of over $15,000, in addition to the large loss of stock and materials.[191]

The Waterloo Organ Company then purchased the old William W. Wood mill site, just south of the organ company's woodworking plant on the west side of Washington Street. On the former mill site, Waterloo built a three-story frame piano building. (This building is currently Moore's Furniture With a Future, at 38 Washington Street.)[192]

The Waterloo Organ Company became "involuntary bankrupt" in 1902, with some alleged fraud involving Francis Bacon of the First National Bank of Waterloo and Alexander C. Reed, president and largest stockholder of the Waterloo Organ Company.[193] Bacon, Leonard Story and other businessmen of the village had made large investments in both the Waterloo Wagon Company and Waterloo Organ and had signed bonds guaranteeing payment of large sums for both companies. During the litigation over the settlement of Waterloo Organ's affairs, the signers of the bonds had to withstand large losses by reason of having so obligated themselves.[194]

The Vough Piano Company was organized in May 1903 by John Becker, Chauncey L. Becker and William C. Vough, with a capital stock of $50,000. The new company purchased the business and plant of the Waterloo Organ Company and continued the manufacture of Malcolm Love and Alexander

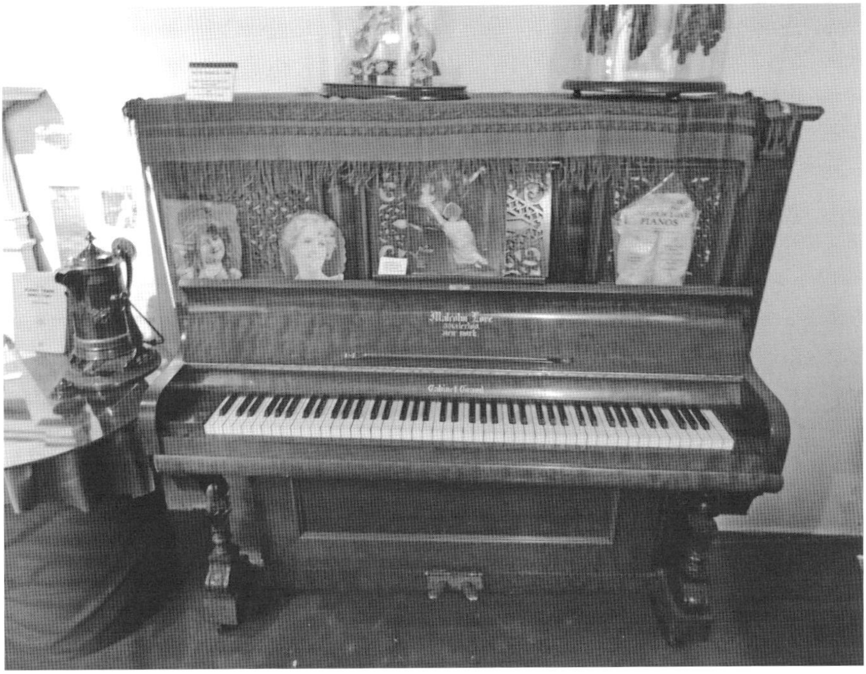

The Waterloo Library and Historical Society has the first manufactured Malcolm Love Piano. *Waterloo Library and Historical Society.*

Pianos, but not organs. The Vough Changeable Pitch Piano, invented by Vough, was featured and widely advertised.[195] This changeable pitch piano was described as "a magnificent, high-grade first-class instrument in all respects, and can be changed instantly by the performer from Standard Pitch to Concert Pitch, and vice versa, simply by 'pushing the button,' thus making this piano suitable for vocal and orchestra work."[196] As many as seven hundred pianos a year were made and sold by the Vough company throughout the eastern United States. In 1913, this business was sold to Wegman Piano Company. In the next decade, the sale of pianos by the company almost ceased.[197]

The large brick building on Washington Street that had been used by the Waterloo Organ Company and later the Vough Piano Company for its woodworking plant was later occupied by the Waterloo Rug Company and the Sussman dress manufactory. On June 23, 1927, there was a fire in the attic near the belfry, but the blaze was extinguished by the fire department. On June 22, 1928, in a spectacular fire, the building was burned to the ground, completely destroyed. It was not rebuilt.[198] Gone was the making of pianos and organs in Waterloo.

16

A Tale of a Whale or, a Whale of a Tale

In 1891, an embalmed whale created some of the biggest publicity in years in the Village of Waterloo. It is a tale of a whale as well as a whale of a tale.

On June 5, 1888, a Captain Nickerson "captured" a big whale about fifteen miles off of Cape Cod. It was brought down by a "boom lance." It weighed seventy-five tons and measured sixty-five feet long.[199]

It was decided that this whale should be "preserved" so that it could be taken on tour. Some 1,500 gallons of fluid were used to "embalm" this huge amount of flesh, at a cost of $3,000.[200] To get a better idea of the monstrous size of this animal, its tongue weighed 3,500 pounds and made 120 gallons of oil.[201] Apparently, only a twenty-two-foot section of the whale was actually prepared for public exhibition. The preserved whale flesh was thoroughly dried and braced internally with wooden ribs so as to retain the size and shape of a whale.[202] The poster for the exhibition in Seneca Falls described this section of the whale as follows: "His Lower Jaw will seat 25 persons. His Mouth has been fitted up as a Reception Room. A person six feet tall can stand erect in his Mouth, between the Monster's Jaws. We have had 25 gentlemen seated in his Mouth, enjoying an oyster supper."[203]

For two years, the embalmed whale—referred to as "His Whaleship"—was exhibited in cities in seven states. "Hundreds of thousands of astonished people" paid an admission to see this great animal—a whale was something that most Americans had never seen. Advertising for the exhibition added that "It is not only a Wonderful Sight, but instructive to Men, Women and

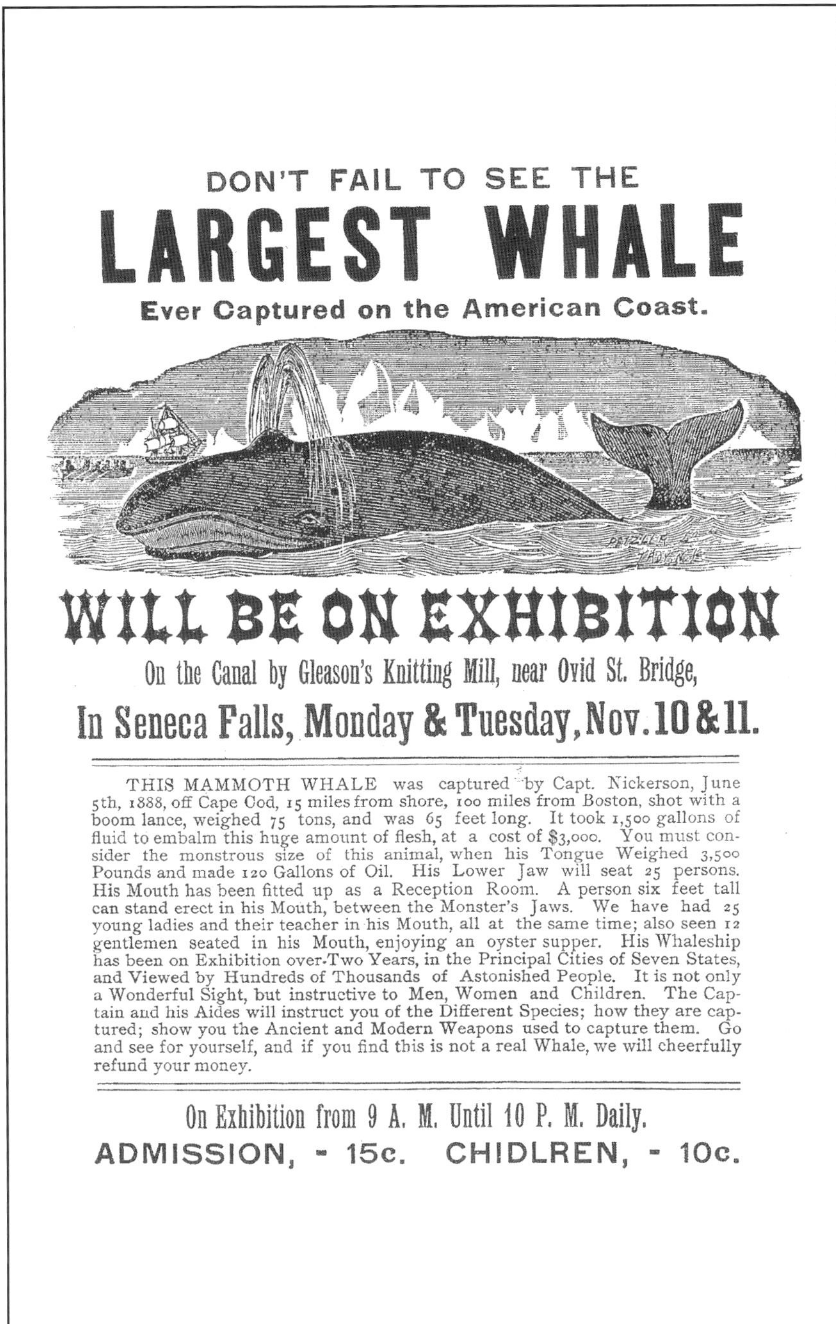

The whale was on display in Seneca Falls before it went to Waterloo. *Seneca County Historian's Office.*

Children. The Captain and his Aides will instruct you of the Different Species; how they are captured; show you the Ancient and Modern Weapons used to capture them. Go and see for yourself, and if you find this is not a real Whale, we will cheerfully refund your money."[204]

The whale was transported on the Erie Canal and displayed at the New York State Fair in Syracuse in 1891. It continued west on the canal to various stops. On November 10 and 11, it was on display at Gleason's Knitting Mill in Seneca Falls. Adults had to pay fifteen cents to get a look, and children paid a dime.[205]

From Seneca Falls, the whale was transported to Waterloo and put on display at the Eagle Tavern. John E. Becker, in his history of Waterloo, provides the following account of what happened to the whale in Waterloo. Throughout the day on November 13 or 14, many paid to see "His Whaleship" and enjoyed doing so. There were, however, a few rowdies who made a demonstration against it early in the evening. They took the wagon on which it was placed out into the street. They threatened to put the whale in the canal to see if it could swim. They didn't actually carry out their threat, however. The whale was taken back to the tavern barn and locked up for the night.

About three o'clock in the morning, nearby people were awakened by a bright light. They soon found out that the whale had been taken from the tavern barn, moved onto the street and set afire. The hostler of the hotel, a Frenchman, ran up to the whale owner's room and cried, "Mr. Parsons, Mr. Parsons, your codfish be all on fire!" Those responsible for dragging the whale out of the barn and burning it were never caught. Becker's account concludes:

> *The Burning of the Whale did more for Waterloo than was intended. The perpetrators contemplated only a little amusement in rebuking a gross imposition, but had the village been the theatre of such a battle and victory as that which has given distinction to her name-sake across the Atlantic, she would have been scarcely more signalized. On the Eastern sea, and beyond the father of western rivers, and in distant southern climes, this unpretending town became known as "the place where the whale burned."*[206]

This whale was the basis for Dick Case's column in the February 21, 2012 edition of the *Syracuse Post-Standard*. Dr. Al Falcone had contacted Case with the question, "Do you remember the whale?" In the hopes of learning about the animal, Case contacted Dan Ward, curator at the Erie Canal Museum, and Pamela Priest, archivist at the Onondaga Historical Association. Ward reported that the whale had been displayed at the state fair in Syracuse before it went on to Seneca Falls. Priest provided Case with a copy of the poster advertising the appearance of the whale in Seneca Falls.[207]

When I saw that article, I contacted Dick Case and provided him with additional information about this whale story. In his April 5, 2012 column, Case told "the rest of the story" with this author's supplied information.[208]

17

The Windmill

Since 1929, "The Windmill" has been a landmark on Routes 5 and 20, just west of Seneca Falls. Roscoe Kean, who had built fifteen cottages along the Cayuga-Seneca Canal, wanted to add a restaurant and other facilities. But not just any simple facility would be satisfactory. Kean "was a real dreamer, an innovator," according to Dick Compo, former executive vice president of the Seneca County Chamber of Commerce. Kean conceived of a windmill that would welcome visitors to "The Windmill Tourist Camp." It was built to authentic one-third scale, using plans Kean had secured in Holland. The Windmill was painted green, and the blades were painted cream. The head carpenter for the construction was Gilbert Melious Sr. of Phelps, with assistance from Martin Hay and Dutch Hurlburt of Gorham.

The front part of the Windmill housed a gasoline station with at least eight pumps. Kean sold a petroleum mixture called "Kean's Purple Flash." It was purple largely because he bought the cheapest gas from many different companies and added a purple dye so that all of his gas would be the same color. He initially sold his product for ten to twelve cents a gallon. The Windmill was heated by a wood-burning stove, which had a chimney that went through the roof.

The back half of the Windmill was divided into men's and women's restrooms, with showers and toilets for guests in the cabins. Cabin guests paid one dollar a night for lodging. To provide water for the showers and toilets, Kean rigged up a ring gear from a Model T Ford and pumped water from the river to a cistern on the second floor of the Windmill.

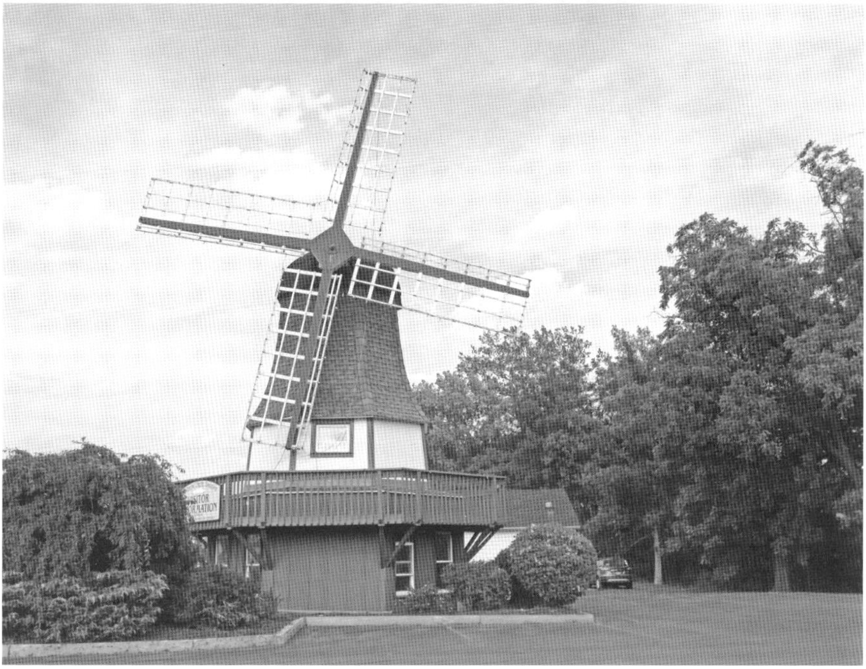

In recent years, "The Windmill" has served as a visitors' information center, operated by the Seneca County Chamber of Commerce. *Walter Gable.*

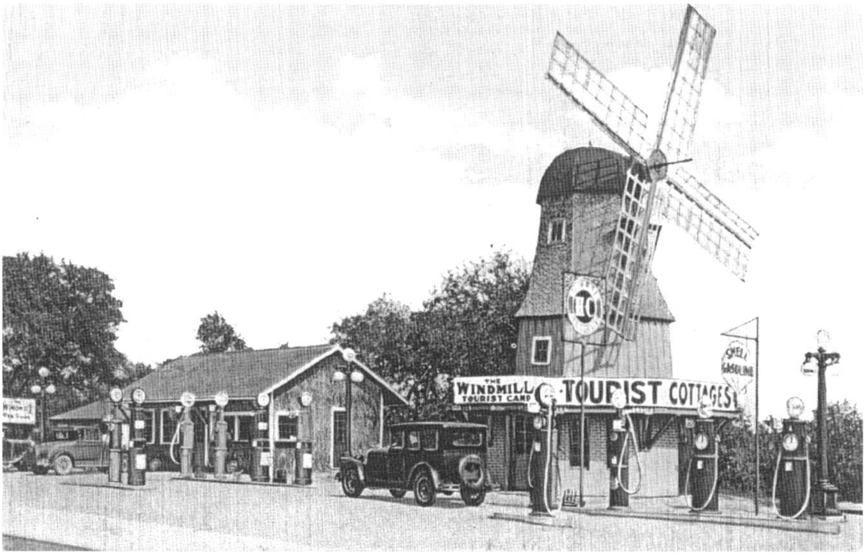

Roscoe Kean built a one-third-scale Dutch windmill to help attract motorists to his gas pumps and overnight tourist cabins. *Seneca County Historian's Office.*

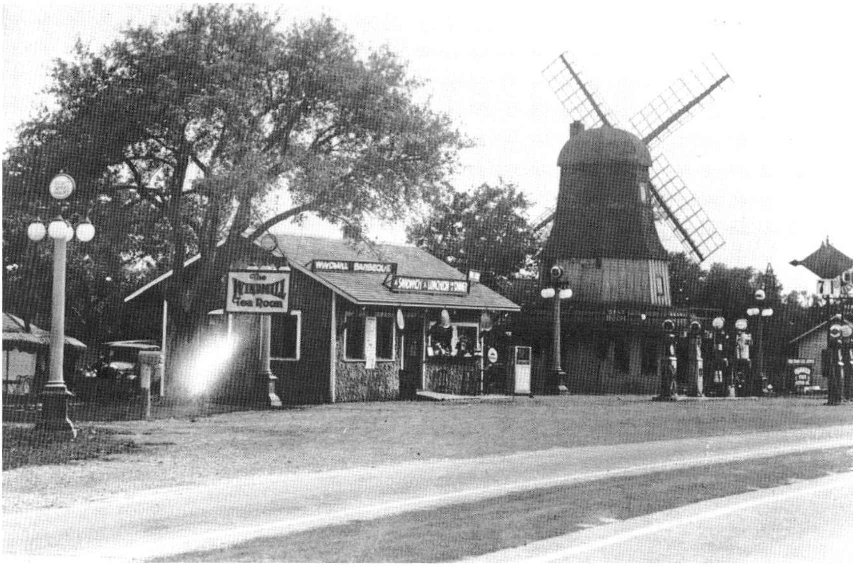

Adjacent to the Windmill, Kean operated a tearoom as another part of the complex. *Seneca County Historian's Office.*

Demonstrating still more innovation, Kean built a pottery and souvenir shop east of the Windmill, selling souvenirs he made out of old wooden crates acquired from nearby grocery stores. In the winter months, when tourism was slow, he used the wood from the crates to make ducks and knicknacks that he then painted and hung by strings. In the Depression year of 1929, he reportedly earned $20,000 from the business.

Shortly after the United States entered World War II, Kean went to work as a civil engineer for Evans Chemetics, making chemicals and pesticides used by the army in Africa. On December 1, 1945, Kean sold the Windmill property to Helen Antoniak and Robert and Mary Irland. Antoniak and the Irlands sold the property to Lee and Hazel Park on October 31, 1951. The Parks in turn sold the property to Mario and Mary Riani on November 29, 1955. They moved the motel offices from the Windmill to their home adjacent to the new motel. The cabins were sold and moved to various locations.

The Windmill was closed until Western Regional Off Track Betting (OTB) leased the property from 1973 to 1979. The OTB used the Windmill for storage and employed a drawing of the structure as the logo for its Seneca County betting parlor.

On June 13, 1980, the Seneca County Chamber of Commerce purchased the Windmill and 120 feet of road frontage. Raising about $39,000 through a community campaign, with major contributions from Goulds Pumps and GTE Sylvania, the chamber renovated the Windmill structure as an office. A crossbeam was installed to support the second floor, and a new circular interior stairway and an external stairway were built. The chamber opened its new offices in October 1980. Chamber executive director Dick Compo told reporters at the time that the chamber bought the Windmill for its offices "because it is a reference point for people within the area. This will give the Chamber a new image. We are preserving a landmark."

Originally, the twenty-foot blades of the Windmill rotated on a steel shaft turned by an electric motor with a freewheeling clutch. The clutch allowed the blades to turn clockwise, but if the wind got too strong, the clutch would switch, and the blades would turn counterclockwise. When the chamber purchased the Windmill, the engine was disconnected, and the blades only turned when the wind blew. Later, because of liability concerns, the blades were stabilized so they wouldn't turn. In April 1991, at a cost of $3,500, a new set of sixteen-foot blades was installed.

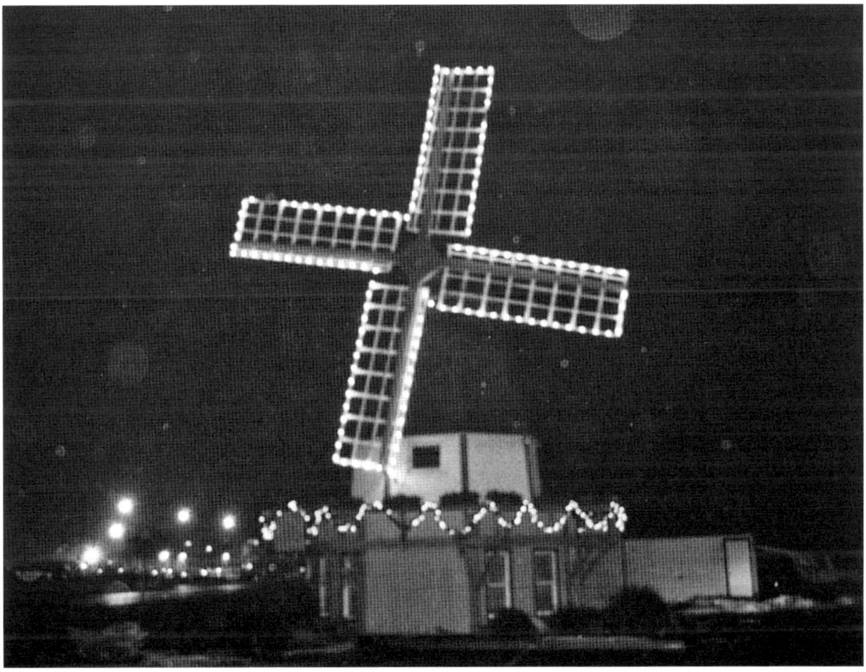

During the holiday season, the Windmill's blades are lit, making a striking sight at night. *Walter Gable.*

When the chamber began planning for its current headquarters (which it moved into in December 1999) adjacent to the Windmill structure, questions about the future of the Windmill loomed large. Some felt that the Windmill had outlived its usefulness and that demolishing it would add parking space for the new headquarters. People with strong ties to the Windmill came forward to ensure its preservation. The most notable efforts and financial support came from the Sessler family members, who were the children of Barbara Park Sessler. She was the daughter of Lee and Hazel Park, who had owned the Windmill from 1951 to 1955. The Windmill today is the Barbara Park Sessler Visitor Center. This use continues the vision of the original builder, who wanted to welcome tourists.

18

Ezra Sutton and the First Home Run in Major League Baseball

Ezra Ballou Sutton, who was born in Seneca Falls, hit the first home run in major-league baseball. Although he has not been inducted into the National Baseball Hall of Fame and Museum, his professional baseball career is noteworthy. His later life was also marked with tragedies.

Sutton was born on Monday, September 17, 1849, in Seneca Falls. His parents were Amos T. and Clarinda Sutton. Ezra was the fifth of their six children. The entire Sutton family was born and raised in New York State. Amos was a flour miller. Seneca Falls at the

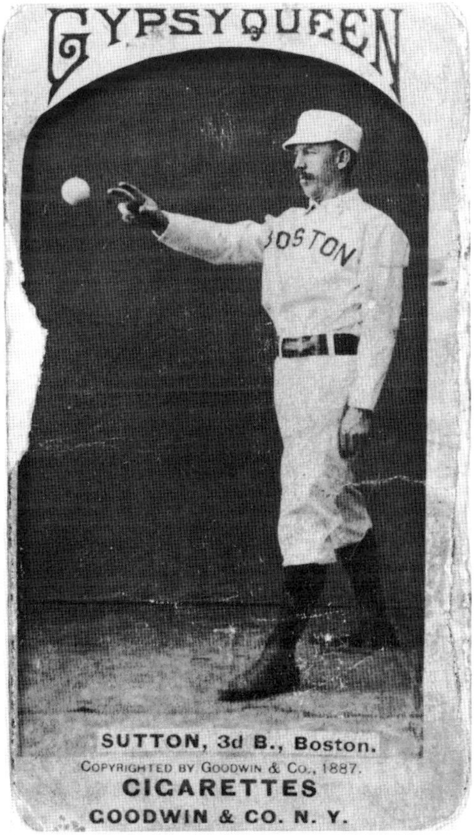

Ezra Sutton, who was born in Seneca Falls, hit the first two home runs in professional major-league baseball. *Walter Gable.*

time was the third-busiest flour milling city in the world, behind only Rochester and Oswego.[209]

Playing for the Rochester Alerts

In his mid- to late teens, Sutton was playing for amateur clubs in and around Rochester. In 1869, he joined the Alerts of Rochester, an amateur member of the National Association of Base Ball Players.[210] Nearly three thousand spectators gathered at Jones Square to watch the Alerts play its opening game on June 4. On the team that day were five players who would go on to play in the nation's first major leagues: John Glenn, Sam Jackson, Eugene Kimball, John McKelvey and Ezra Sutton. Their opponents that day were the Cincinnati Red Stockings, the nation's first team of fully salaried, acknowledged professionals. All members of the Alerts were playing without pay, meaning that most had jobs of some kind. The Alerts lost, 18–9, but that was a smaller loss than Cincinnati had dealt the Niagaras in Buffalo the previous day: 42–6. The Red Stockings seemed to have inspired the Alerts to play better. In July and August, they won all their games, both at home and away, against teams from Oswego, Syracuse, Auburn, Utica and Albany.[211]

In early September, the Alerts made an exhaustive four-day western tour by railroad, with games in Buffalo, Cleveland, Cincinnati and Detroit. Without hotel accommodations, they had to get along with little more sleep than they managed in their train seats. Not surprisingly, they had only one win, a 30–8 victory over the Detroit Citys on September 3. The *Buffalo Express* praised the Alerts as "healthy," "muscular" and "gentlemanly" baseball experts and hailed Ezra Sutton as "the acknowledged third baseman of the country."[212]

The Rochester Alerts played two games in September against the Forest City Club of Cleveland. The Forest City management was so impressed with Sutton that they recruited him for the 1870 season.[213]

By this time, Sutton had already gained a national reputation for his fielding skills. The *Daily Cleveland Herald* supported that status when it reported that Sutton "earned the reputation of being one of the best third basemen in the country."[214] His throwing was remarkable for its swiftness and accuracy.[215]

In 1871, the Cleveland team joined the National Association, baseball's first all-professional league. Sutton remained with this team through the 1872 season.[216]

CONTROVERSY WITH THE PHILADELPHIA ATHLETICS

In 1873, Sutton signed with the Philadelphia Athletics. In July and August 1874, he was part of a group of ballplayers from the Boston and Philadelphia baseball clubs that traveled to England and Ireland to play baseball and cricket. This was the first overseas tour by American baseball players, an attempt by Harry Wright to promote American baseball in his native country.[217] In a throwing match in London on August 13, Sutton carried off second honors by throwing the ball the remarkable distance of 122 yards.[218]

On June 26, 1875, Sutton and teammate Cap Anson were recruited by Albert G. Spalding to join the Chicago White Stockings for the 1876 season. The agreement was made during the playing season, which was illegal under National Association rules, as well as a violation of the ballplayers' contracts. Nevertheless, both Spalding and William Hulbert, the owner of the White Stockings, went ahead with their plans. To get around a charge of "tampering," Hulbert planned a separate league for the 1876 season—the National League. (This National League remains today as the oldest sports league in the United States.) Perhaps bowing to pressure from fans and the ball club in Philadelphia, and perhaps simply because of a promise of increased pay, Sutton reneged on his promise to join the White Stockings.[219] In the 1875 season, he had the best batting average on the Philadelphia Athletics team and the fifth-best average of all professional players in the country.[220] Sutton remained with the Philadelphia Athletics when the team joined the National League in 1876.

Sadly, in that 1876 season, Sutton injured his right arm. His throwing strength was reduced to merely average for the rest of his playing career. For the next few years, Sutton split his playing time between third base and shortstop. He became a master of the so-called trapped play, in which fielders deliberately drop a pop-up, hoping to trap runners off their bases. The National League enacted the "infield fly rule" in 1894 to combat this play.

MAJOR ACCOMPLISHMENTS WITH THE BOSTON RED STOCKINGS

Ezra Sutton joined the Boston Red Stockings in 1877 at a salary of $1,200. He stayed with the team through the 1888 season. He became very popular with Boston fans. The club won the pennant in 1877, 1878 and again in

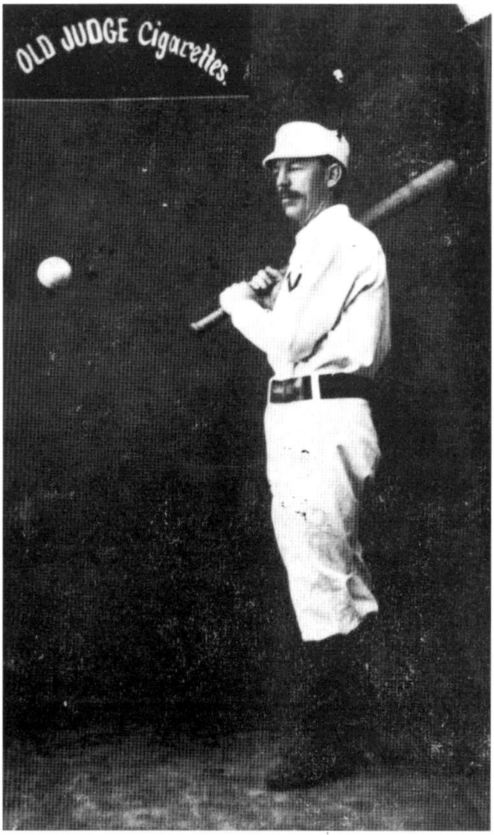

A baseball card showing Ezra Sutton playing third base for the Boston Red Stockings. *Walter Gable.*

1883. In the 1883, '84 and '85 seasons, Sutton batted over .300. In 1883, he was among the league leaders in hits, runs, total bases, RBIs, slugging and on-base percentage. In 1884, he led the National League in hits, was third in batting average and fourth in on-base percentage.

Sutton spent much of the 1886 season in the outfield, not playing every game. Sutton was thirty-five years old, and the third baseman was the younger Billy Nash. Sutton still had some great games, such as the August 27, 1887 contest, when he scored six times against Pittsburgh in a 28–14 romp.

Sutton played his final major-league baseball game on June 20, 1888. Nine days later, he was dropped by Boston, having appeared in just twenty-eight games that season. The Washington Senators expressed interest in picking up Sutton, but management changed its mind. When no other major-league club showed interest in Sutton, the Red Stockings released him outright.

Later Professional Career

On July 10, 1888, Sutton signed with the Rochester club of the International Association. The league had teams in Toronto, Hamilton and London in Ontario, Canada, and in Syracuse, Rochester, Buffalo and Troy in New York.

In May 1889, he was named the player-manager for the Milwaukee team in the Western Association. Sutton was released, however, in mid-July. In May 1890, he signed as player-manager for the Hartford team in the Atlantic Season. The team compiled a 22-60 record and disbanded in August 1890.

Sutton then played sporadically with some semipro and amateur teams. In 1896, he played with a club in Auburn, New York.

Tragedy in His Post-Baseball Years

Sutton and his wife, Susan, married in 1871. They had three children, one of whom died in childhood.

After Sutton was released by Boston in 1888, the family moved permanently to a farm in Palmyra, New York. In 1886, Sutton had gone into the family business, purchasing from his brothers a share in a Palmyra gristmill. When that business failed in 1890, Sutton worked for an ice company for several years.

At some point in the early 1890s, Sutton began to suffer locomotion problems. It was the onset of locomotor ataxia, the inability to control bodily movements. The first symptoms were in his feet, but by the end of the decade, his mobility was severely curtailed. A couple of years later, he was paralyzed in both legs, relying on his family for support and daily care.

On November 26, 1905, Susan Sutton's dress caught fire at the dinner table when a lamp exploded. She suffered severe burns, with her paralyzed husband unable to do anything but watch. Susan died in the hospital six weeks later.

Unable to care for himself, Ezra Sutton was placed in the long-term facility of the Homeopathic Hospital in Rochester. A couple of months later, he sent a letter of appeal for help to Tim Murnane, a former teammate and then a sportswriter for the *Boston Globe*. In that letter, Sutton wrote, "I am at the Homeopathic Hospital in Rochester. I came here April 3 suffering from locomotor ataxia. I cannot go out. My sickness was brought on by overwork. The doctors I used up [*sic*] all my money trying to get cured. My wife was burned to death last January through the explosion of a lamp." Sutton signed the letter "E.B. Sutton, a ball player in distress."[221]

Murnane published parts of the letter on June 11, 1906. Sutton's old friends and teammates started to take up a collection. John Morrill, Sutton's former manager in Boston, personally took up the cause, collecting funds and overseeing Sutton's care. Morrill had Sutton relocated that fall to a state facility in Bridgewater, Massachusetts. As this was near Boston, Morrill could better oversee Sutton's care, and friends and former teammates would be able to visit him. It did mean, however, that Sutton was now farther away from his daughter and two living sons, who were living near Rochester.

Realizing that his end was near and not wanting to die in a state institution, Sutton had himself moved to a private hospital in Braintree, Massachusetts, in June 1907. He died there on June 20 at the age of fifty-seven.[222] Sutton was buried in Palmyra Village Cemetery.

Noteworthy Professional Baseball Accomplishments

Sutton's major-league professional baseball career lasted from 1871 to 1888. In that period, he collected 1,574 hits and had a lifetime batting average of .294. In his two best seasons, 1883 and 1884, he collected 203 runs and 296 hits.

On May 8, 1871, he hit the first home run in professional baseball history while playing for the Cleveland Forest Citys against the Chicago White Stockings. He hit a second home run in that same game, but Cleveland still lost, 14–12.

As third baseman for the Cleveland Forest Citys, he played the first game in the National Association on May 4, 1871. As third baseman for the Philadelphia Athletics, he played in the first game of the National League on April 22, 1876. Sutton was a member of the Boston Red Caps (later redubbed the "Beaneaters"), which won pennants in 1877, 1878 and 1883.

Sutton was among the first several players to collect one thousand hits in the major leagues.[223]

He appeared at bat a total of 5,537 times.[224]

Some Concluding Comments

Ezra Ballou Sutton's later years were marked by the tragic death of his wife and his debilitating condition.

The baseball contract that Sutton signed in the fall of 1879 to play for the Boston Red Stockings in the 1880 season is one of the most well-documented stolen institutional artifacts in history. That is another story—too lengthy for this chapter.

Ezra Sutton had a great professional baseball career. This is especially significant in that it came in the very first years of professional baseball. It seems that he is deserving of consideration for induction into the National Baseball Hall of Fame.

19

The Black Diamond

From 1896 until 1959, the flagship passenger train on the Lehigh Valley Railroad was the Black Diamond Express. Before there were commercial air routes, the fastest way to get from New York City to Buffalo was by train. The Black Diamond became famous for its luxurious passenger cars and its scenic route.

The Lehigh Valley Railroad was one of several anthracite coal railroads that arose in eastern Pennsylvania, New Jersey and New York in the 1850s. In the next few decades, the Lehigh Valley acquired several "short lines." In 1892, the railroad secured its own direct route between the Atlantic Seaboard and Buffalo on Lake Erie, giving it direct access to the Great Lakes, an expanding market for its Pennsylvania coal. Not content with transporting coal and other products, the Lehigh Valley embarked on making a serious bid to capture much of the lucrative New York City–Buffalo passenger business away from the New York Central Railroad and the Delaware, Lackawanna and Western Railroad.[225] The Lehigh Valley Railroad management decided to initiate a luxury express train that could make the trip from Jersey City (the Lehigh's New York metropolitan station) to Buffalo in just over nine and a half hours.[226]

In an effort to generate some national pre-inaugural publicity, the Lehigh Valley conducted a naming contest for this passenger train. Receiving approximately thirty-five thousand entries, railroad management chose the name suggested by Charles M. Montgomery of Toledo, Ohio: Black Diamond Express. Montgomery considered the name "most befitting the premier train

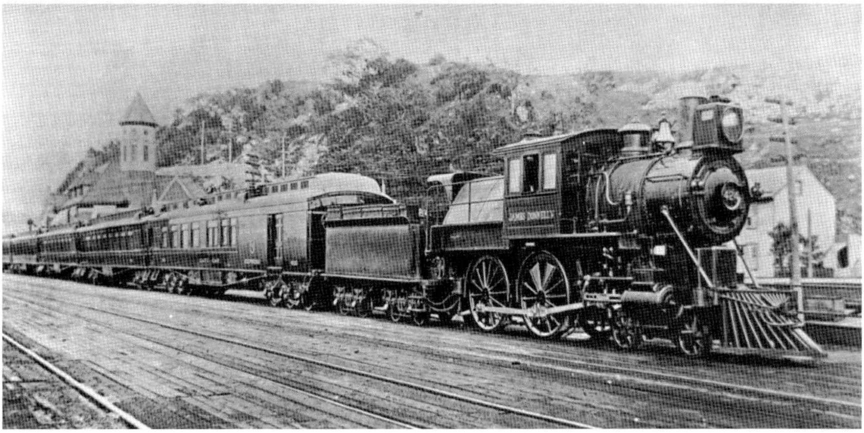

This publicity photo of the Black Diamond Express was taken on May 16, 1896, just two days before the train's inaugural run. *L.L. Jackson Collection.*

of a railroad whose history and revenues were so closely intertwined with anthracite," which had been referred to as "black diamonds." Montgomery received a cash prize of twenty-five dollars.[227]

The Black Diamond Express made its inaugural run on Monday, May 18, 1896.[228] There were actually two trains—the No. 9 was the eastbound train, and the No. 10 was the westbound train. Both left their respective station (Buffalo for No. 9 and Jersey City for No. 10) at noon to travel the 447.6 miles in 613 minutes at an average speed of 44 miles an hour.[229]

Each train consisted of one baggage and library car, two day coaches, a dining car and one Pullman parlor car with an observation end. With the engine, the train itself was about 315 feet long. The Lehigh Valley Railroad was determined to have the train become known as the "Handsomest Train in the World." The cars were purchased from the Pullman Palace Car Company, which was considered the "last word in coachbuilding." An advertisement of the time stated, "Each car on the train is finished in polished Mexican mahogany, with figured mahogany panels and inlaid beveled French plate mirrors. The ceilings are of the new style Empire dome patter, finished in white and gold."[230] The dining car was presided over by chefs. According to railroad advertising, their culinary artistry was expressed in "preparing and serving substantials and delicacies in most appetizing fashion."[231]

The train route consisted of three sections. The first section was from the Jersey City terminal to Easton, Pennsylvania, a distance of 77 miles that was

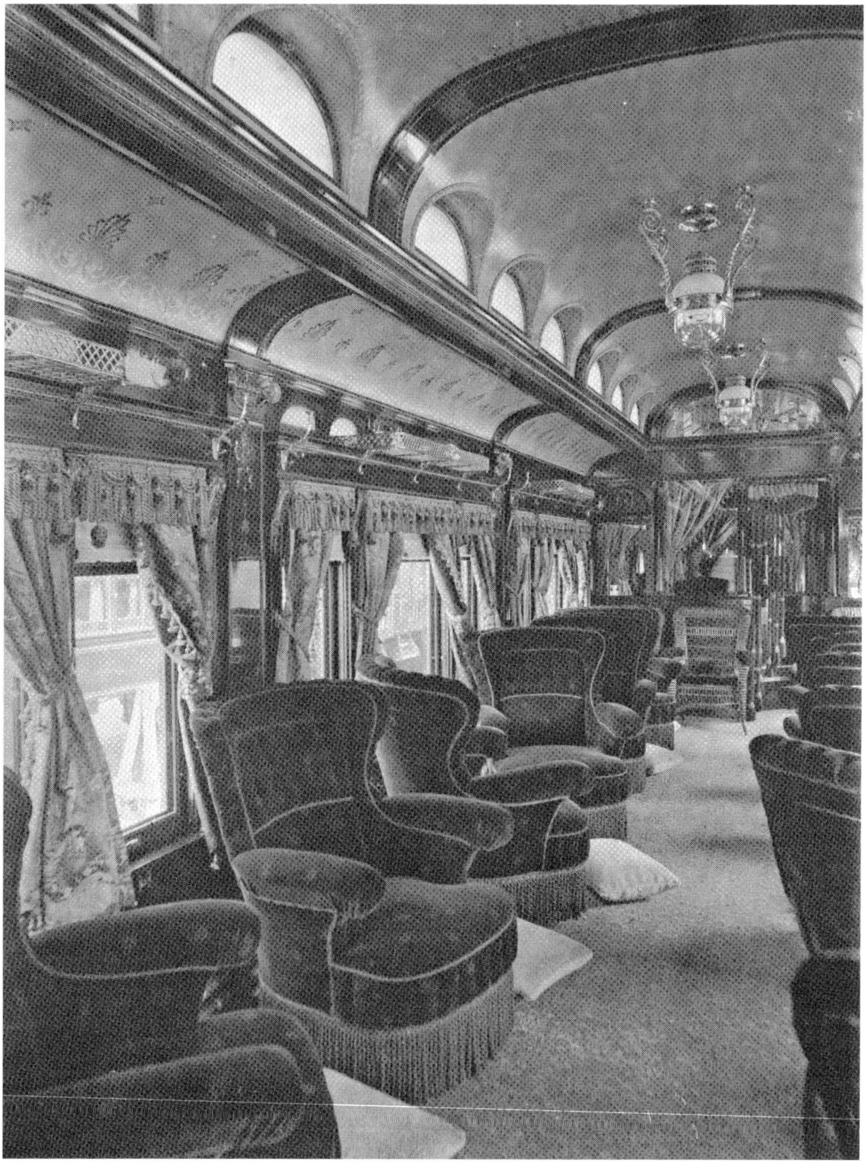

The last car on the Black Diamond train was the parlor observation car, which had a lavishly appointed Victorian decor and an observation platform. *Smithsonian Collection.*

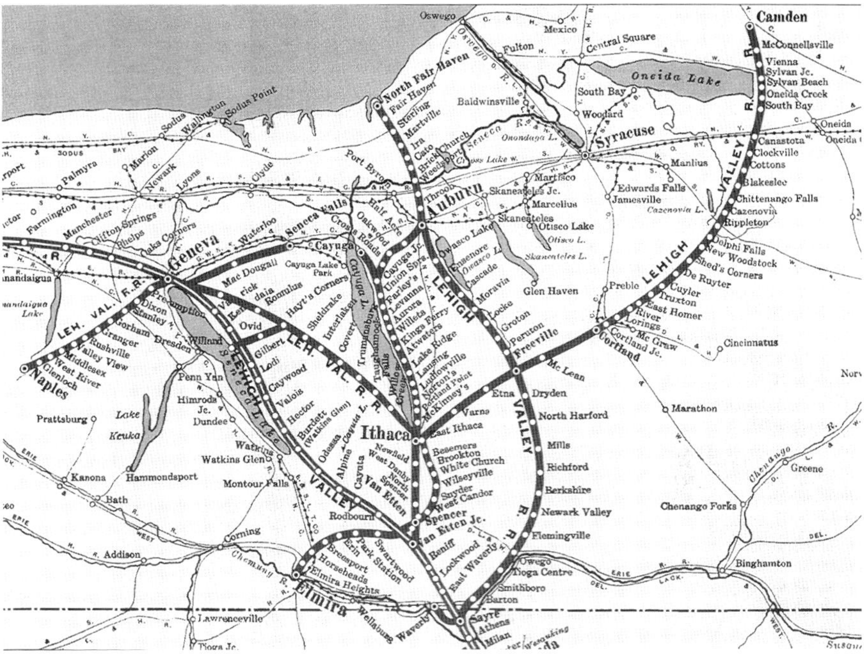

The Black Diamond Express could travel from Sayre, Pennsylvania, to Geneva, New York, via the Ithaca line of the Lehigh Valley Railroad or via the line that traveled inland near the eastern shore of Seneca Lake. *Seneca County Historian's Office.*

to be covered in 96 minutes. The middle section was from Easton to Sayre, Pennsylvania, a distance of 194 miles to be covered in 287 minutes. The third section was from Sayre to Buffalo, New York, a distance of 194 miles to be covered in 230 minutes. The middle section was the longest and the hardest, as the road crossed the mountains, but it was very picturesque for travelers.[232]

The Black Diamond Express passed through Seneca County on its route between stops at Sayre, Pennsylvania, and Geneva, New York. Initially, the Black Diamond traveled via the Seneca Lake freight bypass rather than the Main Line between Ithaca and Geneva Junction (so named because, at that point, the Lehigh Valley and New York Central rails met). This made it possible to avoid the uphill grades out of Ithaca, thus shaving precious minutes from the train's running time. On April 21, 1897, the train made the forty-four-mile stretch between Alpine and Geneva Junction at an average speed of eighty miles per hour. Imagine the eyes of a young lad getting larger and larger as that train sped by so fast![233]

The Black Diamond Express was so popular with Niagara Falls–bound newlyweds that it was nicknamed the "Honeymoon Express." Despite the beauty of the route, the Black Diamond found it difficult to compete with the New York Central's Empire State Express, which could make the run between New York City and Buffalo in two hours less time. In 1908, the Black Diamond was suspended for four months because of sluggish business and rising operating costs. When it was revived, the train was equipped with all-steel dining, club and observation cars. In the summer of 1934, the Black Diamond cars became air conditioned.[234]

The devastating floods of early July 1935 disrupted the operation of the Black Diamond. On the night of July 7, eight and a half inches of rainfall caused major washouts on both the Seneca Lake freight bypass and the main Ithaca Line, paralyzing service to Buffalo. Tracks had been washed away in 287 places, and twenty bridges and culverts were partially or totally wiped out. It was not until July 11 that passenger service was restored via the Ithaca Line. It cost over $500,000 for the Lehigh Valley to restore its operation.[235]

In April 1940, the Black Diamond was refurbished by industrial designer Otto Kuhler. Its new commercial passenger appeal was short-lived. The formal involvement of the United States in World War II, following the Pearl Harbor attack, led to the Lehigh Valley Railroad concentrating on transporting war materials and troops.

Following the war, the Lehigh Valley shifted to diesel engines. The last steam-powered run of the Black Diamond was on May 15, 1948. Unlike most other major eastern railroads, the Lehigh Valley did not change over to new lightweight passenger equipment after the war. This had serious negative implications for the operation, as suggested by this quote: "The worn and, for the most part, antiquated cars were but a threadbare reminder of the palmier days of passenger transport. Particularly painful was the obvious disparity between the obsolete condition of the Black Diamond, the one-time showcase train of the LV, and the rival Lackawanna's sleek new crack train, the Phoebe Snow."[236] The last Black Diamond Express trains ran on May 11, 1959.[237]

Today, the Black Diamond is long gone, along with the Lehigh Valley Railroad's main line to Buffalo. Each year, there are fewer people still alive who can say they fondly remember seeing the Black Diamond as it sped by.

20

The Trial of Rhoda Bement

In the 1840s, at least three reform movements—abolition (antislavery), temperance and women's rights—were evolving in Seneca Falls. The 1843–44 trial of Rhoda Bement by the session of the Presbyterian Church in Seneca Falls clearly shows how these issues were festering and interacting before the 1848 Seneca Falls Convention.

There were tensions between the radical abolitionists and those who were more sympathetic to slavery. On the national political scene, the Democratic Party had been avoiding taking a strong stand on the slavery issue in an attempt to keep the party from being split north and south. Various churches, including the Methodist and Presbyterian

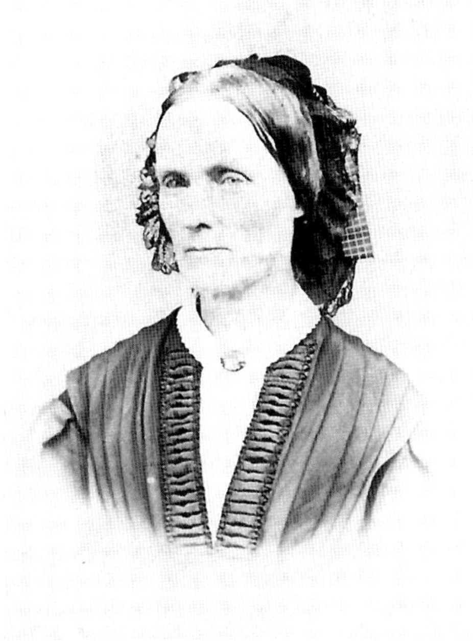

In 1844, Rhoda Bement was censured and expelled as a member of the Presbyterian Church in Seneca Falls. In 2013, the local church session overturned that censure. *Frances Pepper.*

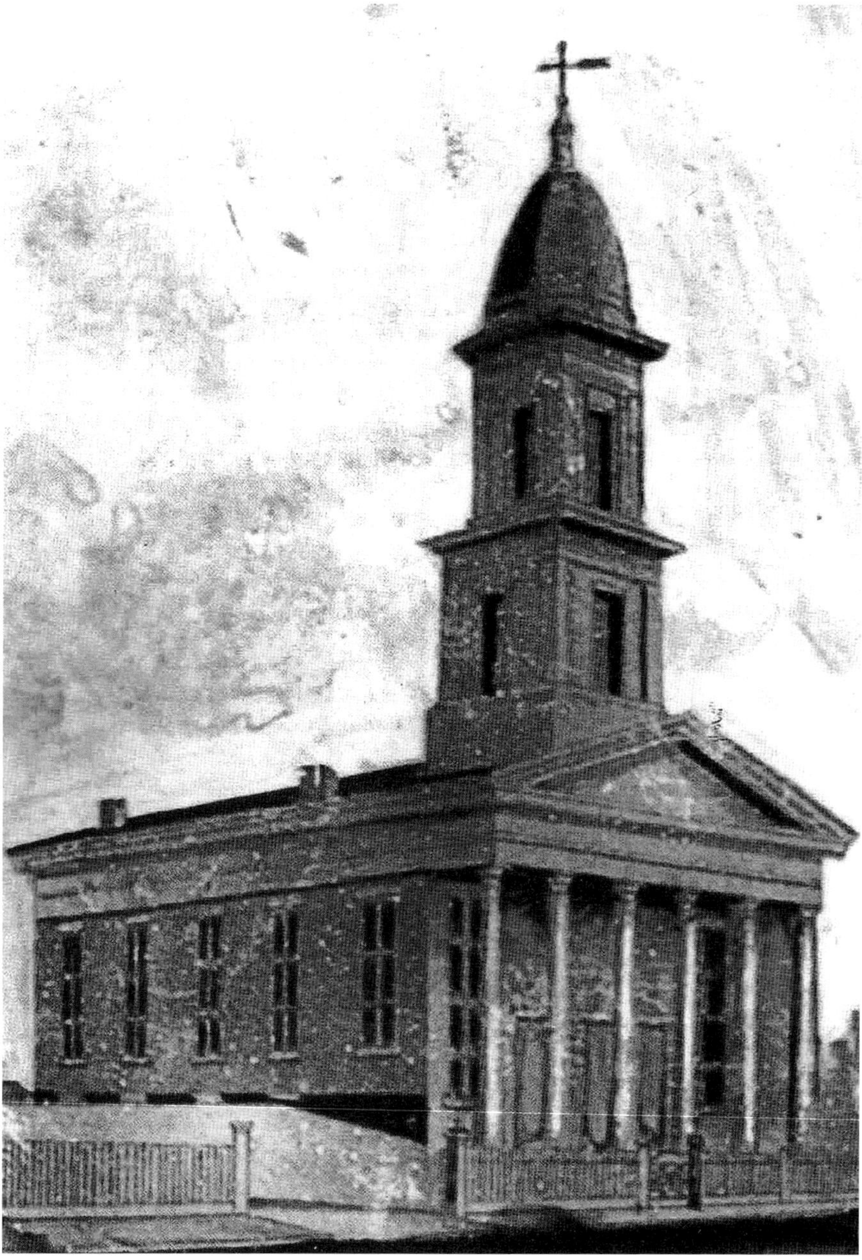

This was the Seneca Falls Presbyterian Church building in the 1840s. *Seneca Falls Historical Society.*

denominations, had not taken a definitive position on slavery, in the hopes of keeping all church members throughout the nation united. The local Methodist and Presbyterian congregations, similarly, were trying to avoid taking a strong stand either for or against slavery, but this was becoming increasingly difficult.

Abby Kelley in Seneca Falls

In August 1842, Abby Kelley gave several public "lectures" in Seneca Falls. This was part of her extensive travels throughout upstate New York as an agent for the Western New York Anti-Slavery Society. She denounced even northern churches if they were not antislavery. Even taking a neutral position on slavery—neither publicly for nor against it—was unacceptable to her. She repeatedly denounced "colonizationists" (those who favored freeing slaves and sending them back to Africa). Because the Reverend Horace P. Bogue, acting pastor of the Presbyterian church in Seneca Falls, had been an agent for the American Colonization Society, Abby Kelley had no real respect for him. Similarly, it should not be surprising that Reverend Bogue would be less than sympathetic to abolitionists in his own congregation, fearing that their extreme position on slavery would lead to division within the congregation. Immediately after Kelley's lectures in Seneca Falls in 1842, Bogue had the Presbyterian Church conduct inquiries about any Presbyterians who had attended her lectures. Ansel Bascom reported that those conducting these perfunctory inquiries were "satisfied with any kind of apology…and put no body upon trial."[238]

No Seneca Falls church would allow Abby Kelley the use of its facilities when she returned for another speaking engagement in August 1843. So she spoke in the apple orchard belonging to Ansel and Eliza Bascom, a site community residents had become accustomed to visiting for events and celebrations, including the Fourth of July. Specifically, Kelley had this to say: "This nation is guilty of slavery. It is a sin. Your churches are connected with slavery, and they are guilty of that sin. They are not Christians if they are slaveholders, if they steal and sell men, women and children, if they rob cradles. Northern churches were as guilty, in fact, as southern slaveholders, since northerners had the majority population and could make things right. That includes your Presbyterian Church." She went on, "I happen to know something of your Mr. Bogue, the pastor of that church. Where is your

Bogue today? Is he not connected with the South? Is he not in full fellowship with proslavery churchmen? These proslavery persecutions today follow the same spirit of persecution that existed in former ages. Mr. Bogue would see me burn at the stake, if he had it in his power, or murdered as abolitionists had been at the south."[239] It is important to understand that she was making these comments on a Sabbath afternoon, at a time when the Presbyterian church was holding its second service. For Rhoda Bement and other church parishioners to hear Abby Kelley speak, they had to, in effect, skip their own church's afternoon service.

BEMENT BECOMES AN ABOLITIONIST ACTIVIST

Abby Kelley's speeches in 1842 and 1843 motivated Rhoda Bement and other Seneca Falls residents to become abolitionist activists—an extreme position referred to at the time as "ultraism." Bement had been a Baptist, but she became a member of the Presbyterian church in Seneca Falls in 1839.[240] Many antislavery fairs were held in Seneca Falls to raise funds to help "freedom seekers" Elizabeth M'Clintock of Waterloo and Bement organized an antislavery fair, held at the Temperance Hall in Seneca Falls on October 4–5, 1843. They advertised "a most beautiful variety of useful and fancy articles, many of which have been contributed from Rochester, Syracuse, Utica, Albany, Boston and many other places." Admittance was half a shilling (about six and one-fourth cents). In the evening, speeches, vocal music and a concert by the Geneva Band afforded a rare "feast of reason and flow of soul." Significantly, this was the first recorded example of Seneca Falls and Waterloo women working together.[241]

According to Rhoda Bement, tensions between Reverend Horace P. Bogue, acting pastor of the Presbyterian church, and herself came into the open in the vestibule of the church on the first Sunday in October 1843. Following the conclusion of the morning worship service, she confronted Bogue privately with a grievance. She said that he had ignored antislavery notices that she had laid on his desk that morning and the previous Sunday, September 24. What began as a conversation ended in a shouting match that was overheard by many parishioners. Bement claimed that Bogue denied that he had seen any notices. Each made accusations against the other. Reverend Bogue accused Bement of being "very unchristian, very impolite and very much out of your place to pounce upon me in this manner." Bement said she had a right to ask him why he hadn't read the notices, especially when he claimed that he was an abolitionist. She is believed to have said to him, "You told me you was an abolitionist and I supposed if you was you would read abolition notices."

CHARGES AGAINST BEMENT

Following the second worship service on October 1, Reverend Bogue met with the church elders, who decided to put Rhoda Bement on trial before the church session. Other charges against Bement suddenly surfaced. One new charge alleged not only that she had acted in an unchristian manner toward Reverend Bogue in the vestibule, but that she had also refused to attend communion and other meetings officiated by Bogue. Another new charge was that she had, "in a conspicuous manner," attended the "exhibition made by Abby Kelley on the first Sabbath of Aug. last…while the church to which Mrs. Bement belongs were attending upon divine service."[242] The session on December 18, 1843, adopted this charge with five specifications:

> *Mrs. Rhoda Bement is charged with disorderly & unchristian conduct.*
>
> - *First in dividing the Lord's Supper, partaking the bread & refusing the cup.*
> - *Second in attending in a conspicuous manner upon the exhibitions made by Abby Kelley on the first Sabbath of Aug. last between the hours of five and eight o'clock P.M. & while the church to which Mrs. Bement belongs were attending upon divine service.*
> - *Third in her behavior towards the Pastor of this church in the vestibule of the church on the first Sabbath of October last in the presence of various members of the congregation.*
> - *Fourth in absenting herself from the communion on said first Sabbath of October.*
> - *Fifth in having absented herself from public worship since that time whenever the acting Pastor of said church has officiated.*[243]

On that same date, the Reverend Samuel H. Gridley, pastor of the Waterloo Presbyterian Church, assumed the role of moderator for all future trial sessions. Gridley denied Bement's request that her husband, Jeremy, be her counsel.[244] Daniel W. Forman served initially as her counsel.[245] On January 23, 1844, Forman withdrew as Bement's counsel because of ill health. He was replaced by Dr. Joseph Kerr Brown.[246]

The Trial

Bement's session trial lasted two full months. The church elders were H. McAlister, A.S. Platt, D.W. Forman, C. Hood, M.C. Deming and J.K. Brown.[247] Dozens of witnesses testified. Manuscript minutes of the proceedings filled sixty pages in the church record book. In her book *The Road to Seneca Falls*, Judith Wellman writes, "Seneca Falls riveted its attention on temperance, abolitionism and woman's rights. Some of the testimony must have made Bogue's supporters regret that they had ever raised these issues."

Regarding her refusal to take wine at communion, Bement argued in her defense that it was not pure "juice of the grape"—it seemed contaminated by "alcohol or some kind of drug." She argued that it was too strong for a person with temperance principles. Others testified in her defense. Delia Matthews stated that "the last time I partook of the wine it was very offensive; it was very strong alcoholic wine. I have been absent the last two communions and at the two previous communions I refused to partake of it." Joseph Metcalf, the key organizer of the Wesleyan Church in Seneca Falls, testified that Methodists saw no need to serve wine as their communion drink. For the past year, they had used unfermented grape juice, boiled and diluted.[248]

Most of the trial focused on Kelley's abolitionism. Bement strongly defended Kelley's comments as being truly Christian. Opponents viewed Kelley's actions differently. They were particularly upset that Kelley had been urging people to sign a "Tea Total Pledge" that summarized the radical abolitionist position. Signers of the pledge asserted that they agreed that slavery was a "heinous sin and crime, a curse to the master and a grievous wrong to the slave." Another part of the pledge statement included, "We will never vote for any candidate for civil office, nor countenance any man as a Christian minister, nor hold connexion [*sic*] with any organization as a christian [*sic*] church" unless political parties and churches refused to support "any provision of the Constitution of the United States in favor of slavery." Signers publicly pledged themselves to "immediate and unconditional emancipation." Signers disavowed all fellowship with those who claimed slaves (ownership of slaves) or with those who voted for "slave claimants or their abettors." Signers of the pledge agreed not to support those who might attempt to put down forcible slave resistance.

The trial testimony about the pledge made many of Bogue's supporters squirm. When Fanny Sackett was asked why she did not sign the pledge, she confessed, "I thought I would be bound to withdraw from the church & did not like to do so." Ansel Bascom said that he felt Kelley's speeches led him to believe that if a person signed the pledge, that person would have to "come out" of all proslavery churches. He said that he considered the Presbyterian Church to be a proslavery church. Cornelia Perry testified that Abby Kelley's August 1842 talks had been the first abolitionist discussion she had ever heard. Perry said, "Our ministers had never told us anything about it & I had supposed there was no very great sin in it."[249]

Woman's rights also were at issue in this trial. "In her challenge to male religious authority, Bement provided a powerful role model." The trial authorities asked Jabez Matthews whether he considered it proper and "clearly established in the Bible…for a female to call a promiscuous meeting for the purpose of addressing them on Moral & Religious subjects," even when it was "contrary to the established sentiment of the church to which they belong."[250] Matthews replied, "I believe it is."[251]

The Verdict

On January 23, 1844, the elders of the church session found Bement guilty of "disorderly and unchristian conduct." The vote of each of the five "specifications" was unanimous, except that Daniel Forman voted "no" on the third specification.[252] A committee consisting of Reverend Gridley, M.B. Bellows and M.C. Deming was appointed to visit Bement to see if she would now see "the error of her ways."[253]

The committee reported to the session on January 30, 1844, that it had been unable to convince Bement. She then appeared at the session and made this statement: "I have but one thing to say. For if I be an offender or have committed any thing worthy of death I refuse not to die; but if there be none of these things whereof they accuse me, no man may deliver me unto them—I appeal not unto Caeser but unto God." She left, and then Forman presented some kind of written dissent and protest as to what the session was likely to do next. The contents of this written document no longer exist. Then the session voted that "Mrs. Bement be suspended from the Communion of this Church until she give evidence of repentance and return to duty."[254] This censure by the session would not be lifted unless she repented. She unsuccessfully appealed the decision to the regional committee of ministers and elders that met at Waterloo a week later.

AFTER THE TRIAL

Presbyterians in Seneca Falls had sustained Reverend Bogue's good name, but they paid a price. The Bements and other abolitionist members left the Presbyterian Church, with many joining the new Wesleyan Church. Those who joined the Wesleyan Church included elder Daniel W. Forman, Sally Freeland Pitcher and Harriet Freeland Lindsley.[255] When the Presbyterian Church session learned that Bement was attending services at the Wesleyan Methodist Church, it voted to excommunicate her.[256] In 1849, the Bements decided to leave Seneca Falls. They moved to Michigan. On the way, Jeremy Bement contracted cholera in Buffalo and died.[257]

IMPLICATIONS OF THE VERDICT

The Rhoda Bement trial showed the extent to which reform sentiments were evolving in Seneca Falls by the fall of 1843. Bement was only one of many Seneca Falls residents who had embraced temperance sentiments by that time. It would be just five years later—in 1848—that both antislavery sentiments and women's rights ideas would result in major action in Seneca Falls. In the case of antislavery sentiments, there were several local meetings to form a Free Soil Party, the goal of which was to keep lands gained from the Mexican-American War from becoming slave states. For the cause of women's rights, important action included the momentous July 1848 Seneca Falls convention. Bement's trial was a clear foreshadowing of these events.

According to Glenn Altschuler and Jan Saltzbager, authors of *Revivalism, Social Conscience and Community in the Burned-Over District*, the central theme of the Rhoda Bement trial is the stress that it generated by the desires for both change and stability.

> *Her challenge to the authority of the male leadership of her church confronted Seneca Falls's Presbyterians with the threat of disunity at a time when harmony was perceived as vital to preserving the influence of the church in the community. The church men and women of Seneca Falls recognized the danger of disintegration in a village already subject to considerable stress and thought of themselves as a nexus of good order. Faced with a threat to harmony, the authorities of the church drew back from activism. Choosing caution, the Reverend Horace Bogue reluctantly brought his parishioner to trial.*[258]

It is easy to think of *current* examples of "stress that is generated by the desires for both change and stability"—here in Seneca County, in the Middle East and in other areas of the world. Hopefully, the Rhoda Bement trial provides us with a perspective to bring to these times of stress.

More to the Story

The story does not end here, however. On February 22, 2013, this author presented a program on local Underground Railroad activity to staff at the New York State Agricultural Station in Geneva, New York. In the audience was Robert Seem, a member of the Seneca Falls Presbyterian Church. He heard me tell about the Rhoda Bement incident in my presentation. He brought that information back to his church and suggested that this censure be overturned. In consultation with the national church organization, Seneca Falls Presbyterian Church officials learned that it would be permissible for a local church session to do so. Accordingly, on September 23, 2013, the local session voted to overturn the 1840s censure of Rhoda Bement. The current pastor, the Reverend Leah Ntuala, said, "I think Rhoda would be dancing with joy in heaven to learn the censure placed on her has been overturned. The church where she once worshiped is now a Covenant Network Church and has for the first time called a female pastor who is married to a black man. God does always have the last laugh." It's as if the Rhoda Bement trial story has come full circle over 150 years later!

Notes

Chapter 1

1. *History of Seneca Co., New York*, 31.
2. Ibid.
3. Ibid., 30–32.
4. Willers, *Centennial Historical Sketch of the Town of Fayette*, 20.

Chapter 2

5. E-mail of October 12, 2016, from Sharon Secor to Seneca County historian Walter Gable.
6. *1981 Seneca County Directory.*

Chapter 3

7. Morrison, *New York State Agricultural College.*
8. Ibid.
9. *Pictorial Album of the Willard Asylum, 1869–1886.*

Chapter 4

10. Casstevens, "Ford Model T."
11. Becker, *History of the Village of Waterloo*, 341.
12. Ibid., 334.

13. Ibid., 343.
14. Information and photos provided by the Seneca Falls Historical Society from its documents collections.
15. *Seneca Falls (NY) Reveille*, May 30, 1913.
16. Elizabeth Auten, "Tin Lizzies," *Seneca County History Newsletter* 1, no. 4 (June 1985): 14.
17. Information provided by Dennis Kenyon of N.R. Boyce car dealership in Ovid, New York, on October 31, 2008. Photos taken by Seneca County historian Walter Gable.
18. August 1, 2016 e-mail from Andrew Herrala to Seneca County historian Walter Gable.
19. Becker, *History of the Village of Waterloo*, 351.
20. Ibid., 354.
21. Ibid.
22. Ibid., 359.
23. Readers are encouraged to see the full article on "The Windmill" and additional photos in the county historian's portion of the Seneca County website, www.co.seneca.ny.us.
24. Information supplied by Seneca County clerk Christina Lotz, http://www.nydmv.state.ny.us/Statistics/statli07.htm.
25. Information supplied by Seneca County clerk Christiana Lotz.

CHAPTER 5

26. Comments made by LouAnn Wurst, associate professor and chair, department of anthropology, SUNY College at Brockport, in a January 23, 2009 e-mail to Allan Buddle, Christine Ridarsky, David Lacy, Kari Lusk and Walter Gable.
27. Ibid.
28. http://home.htva.net/~townofhector/HGrazingAssoc.html.
29. Information taken from the Backbone Ridge History Group brochure.
30. Talking points prepared by Kari Lusk of the Finger Lakes National Forest.
31. Ibid.
32. Information basically quoted from the website of the Finger Lakes National Forest, http://www.fs.fed.us/r9/forests/greenmountain/htm/fingerlakes.
33. Comments by Wurst, January 23, 2009, e-mail to Allan Buddle, Christine Ridarsky, David Lacy, Kari Lusk and Walter Gable.
34. "Archaeology Students Digging at FL Forest," *Finger Lakes (NY) Times*, July 6, 2008.
35. Information taken from the first Backbone Ridge History Group brochure.
36. E-mail from Allan Buddle on March 16, 2016.

CHAPTER 6

37. "Cayuga Lake Park," *Seneca Falls* (NY) *Reveille*, May 26, 1886
38. "The Lake Railroad," *Seneca Falls (NY) Reveille*, 1885 (exact date unknown).
39 "New Street Railroad," *Seneca Falls (NY) Reveille*, January 22, 1886
40. Watrous, *County Between the Lakes*, 141.
41. "The Lake Railroad," *Seneca Falls (NY) Reveille*.
42. Watrous, *County Between the Lakes*, 137.
43. Ibid., 141–43.
44. Ibid., 143–44.
45. Ibid., 144.
46. Ibid., 144–45.
47. Ibid., 160.
48. Ibid., 145–46.
49. King, *Trolleys to Cayuga Lake Park*.
50. Watrous, *County Between the Lakes*, 145–47.
51. Ibid., 148.
52. Ibid., 149–51.
53. Ibid., 151.
54. Ibid.
55. Ibid., 151–52.
56. Ibid., 156.
57. Ibid., 157.
58. Ibid.
59. Ibid., 158.
60. Ibid.
61. Ibid., 159.
62. Ibid., 161.
63. Telephone conversation with Christine Mercy, Cayuga Lake State Park staff member, on March 6, 2008.
64. Watrous, *County Between the Lakes*, 154–55.
65. Ibid., 161.
66. Reserve America, http://www.reserveamerica.com/camping/Cayuga_Lake_State_Park/r/campgroundDetails.

CHAPTER 7

67. Freeman and Freeman, *Cobblestone Quest*, 7.
68. Shelgren, Lattin and Frasch, *Cobblestone Landmarks*, 1.
69. Freeman and Freeman, *Cobblestone Quest*, 7.
70. Shelgren, Lattin and Frasch, *Cobblestone Landmarks*, 4.
71. Klees, *More Legends and Stories of the Finger Lakes Region*, 146–49.
72. Freeman and Freeman, *Cobblestone Quest*, 8.
73. Klees, *More Legends and Stories of the Finger Lakes Region*.

74. Freeman and Freeman, *Cobblestone Quest*, 12.
75. Ibid., 8.
76. Klees, *More Legends and Stories of the Finger Lakes Region.*
77. Freeman and Freeman, *Cobblestone Quest*, 8.
78. Ibid., 12.
79. Ibid., 8.
80. Klees, *More Legends and Stories of the Finger Lakes Region*, 146–49.
81. Freeman and Freeman, *Cobblestone Quest*, 8.
82. Ibid., 13.
83. Ibid., 9.
84. Ibid., 7.
85. Shelgren, Lattin and Frasch, *Cobblestone Landmarks*, 1.
86. Ibid., 7.
87. Ibid., 9.
88. Ibid., 9–10.
89. Ibid., 10.
90. Ibid., 10–11.
91. Klees, *More Legends and Stories of the Finger Lakes Region*, 146–49.
92. Freeman and Freeman, *Cobblestone Quest*, 13–14.
93. Ibid., 12.
94. Ibid.
95. Ibid., 11–12.
96. Klees, *More Legends and Stories of the Finger Lakes Region*, 146–49.
97. Ibid.
98. Shelgren, Lattin and Frasch, *Cobblestone Landmarks*, 25–27.
99. Klees, *More Legends and Stories of the Finger Lakes Region*, 146–49.
100. Shelgren, Lattin and Frasch, *Cobblestone Landmarks*, 1.
101. Freeman and Freeman, *Cobblestone Quest*, 7.
102. Delavan, *Landmarks of Seneca County*, 32.
103. Ibid., 35.
104. Ibid., 40.
105. Ibid., 46.
106. Ibid., 47.
107. Ibid., 49.
108. Ibid., 50.
109. Ibid., 51.
110. Ibid., 56.
111. Ibid., 57.
112. Ibid., 97.
113. Ibid., 155.
114. Klees, *More Legends and Stories of the Finger Lakes Region*, 146–49.
115. Ibid.

CHAPTER 8

116. Howard Hobbs, "Fresno Junior College Imperative," June 1, 1989, http://www.buillldognews.net/fresno-junior-college.html.
117. Brown, *20th Century Biographical Dictionary*.
118. Merrill, "William Watts Folwell."
119. Ibid.
120. "William Watts Follwell, 1869–1884," http://president.umn.edu/about/presidential-history/william-watts-follwell.
121. "William Watts Folwell," Wikipedia, http://en.wikipedia.org/wiki/William_Watts_Folwell.

CHAPTER 9

122. "The Usher-Hunt 'Wells Barn,'" manuscript article of the Interlaken Historical Society.
123. "Granville, New York," Wikipedia, http://en.wikipedia.org/wiki/Granville,_New_York.
124. "The Usher-Hunt 'Wells Barn,'" manuscript article.
125. Information taken from an e-mail from Allan Buddle, former president of the Interlaken Historical Society, dated March 31, 2010.
126. Information found in Robinson, *Sheldrake, 1789–1962*, 34. Herbert Usher was the last of Fred Usher's grandsons to live in the house. Herbert died in the spring of 2012.
127. "The Usher-Hunt 'Wells Barn,'" manuscript article.

CHAPTER 10

128. *Encyclopedia of New York State*, s.v. "Ku Klux Klan," 847.
129. Information found in the KKK folder in the Memorial Day Museum archives of the Waterloo Library and Historical Society.
130. Ibid.
131. E. Thayles Emmons, "Was Klan Ever Active in Geneva?—Here's the History," *Geneva (NY) Times*, August 28, 1965.
132. "Police Ordered on Duty for Klan Parade," *Geneva (NY) Daily Times*, Saturday, September 3, 1927.
133. "Street Riot Mars Parade of the Ku Klux Klan," *Geneva (NY) Daily Times*, September 6, 1927.
134. "Rev. K.A. Bray Attacks Klan in Sermons," *Geneva (NY) Daily Times*, circa December 7, 1923.

CHAPTER 11

135. Becker, *History of the Village of Waterloo*, 53.
136. Rogers, *Forgotten Stories of the Finger Lakes*, 91.
137. Ibid.
138. Becker, *History of the Village of Waterloo*, 53.
139. *Grip's Historical Souvenir of Seneca Falls, N.Y.*, 71.
140. Rogers, *Forgotten Stories of the Finger Lakes*, 91.
141. "'The Kingdom': Once Thriving Little Known," *Shortsville (NY) Enterprise*, November 27, 1924.
142. Ibid.
143. Information taken from the genealogical index cards prepared for former Seneca County historian Betty Auten.
144. Samuel Birdsall studied law with Martin Van Buren. Samuel Birdsall's son Samuel became the private secretary of U.S. secretary of state William H. Seward.
145. *Discovering the Underground Railroad, Abolitionism and African American Life in Seneca County, New York, 1820–1880*, 162.
146. *History of Seneca Co., New York*, 135.
147. At this place on the Seneca River, a lock with a fall of four to five feet had been constructed for navigation around the rapids (*Grip's Historical Souvenir of Seneca Falls, N.Y.*, 7).
148. Rogers, *Forgotten Stories of the Finger Lakes*, 92.
149. "'The Kingdom.'"
150. Ibid.
151. *Grip's Historical Souvenir of Seneca Falls, N.Y.*, , 8.
152. Becker, *History of the Village of Waterloo*, 53.
153. Ibid., 73.
154. Ibid., 78.
155. *Grip's Historical Souvenir of Seneca Falls, N.Y.*, 7–8.
156. *Lowell Daily Courier*, August 13, 1846.
157. *Grip's Historical Souvenir of Seneca Falls, N.Y.*, 15.
158. "'The Kingdom.'"
159. Rogers, *Forgotten Stories of the Finger Lakes*, 92.

CHAPTER 12

160. *History of Seneca County New York*, 17.
161. Morrison, *Town & Village of Ovid*, 16.
162. Becker, *History of the Village of Waterloo*, 117–18. Unless otherwise noted, the information for this article basically comes from this source.
163. Genealogy information provided by Tanya Warren of the Waterloo Historical Society.
164. *Seneca Falls (NY) Reveille*, January 14, 1887.
165. "Summing Up," *Auburn (NY) Bulletin*, April 5, 1887.

166. *Seneca Falls (NY) Reveille*, January 14, 1887.
167. "Trial for Murder," *Syracuse (NY) Weekly Express*, April 6, 1887.
168. Becker, *History of the Village of Waterloo*, 276–77. Note that this is the source for most of the information in this article, except for the information that is specifically cited by subsequent endnotes.
169. Most of this trial information comes from the April 6, 1887 issue of the *Syracuse (NY) Weekly Express*.
170. *Seneca Falls (NY) Reveille*, January 14, 1887.
171. Register No. 385 in *Register of Deaths in the Village of Waterloo, County of Seneca, State of New York*, book at the Clerk's Office, Village of Waterloo.
172. *Auburn (NY) Bulletin*, November 14, 1888.
173. *Seneca Falls (NY) Reveille*, January 14, 1887.
174. *Auburn (NY) Bulletin*, January 13, 1887.
175. "Summing Up," *Auburn (NY) Bulletin*, April 5, 1887.
176. Trial testimony quoted from article in the *Syracuse (NY) Weekly Express*, April 6, 1887.
177. "Murder in the First Degree," *Seneca County (NY) Courier*, April 7, 1887.
178. "Execution of Johnson," *Seneca County (NY) Courier*, November 15, 1888.
179. *Seneca Falls (NY) Reveille*, January 14, 1887.
180. Ibid., January 21, 1887.
181. "Deputy Not Forgotten," *Finger Lakes (NY) Times*, April 13, 2015.
182. DeathPenaltyInfo.org, http://www.deathpenaltyinfo.org/node/1416.
183. "Deputy Not Forgotten," *Finger Lakes (NY) Times*, April 13, 2015.

Chapter 13

184. Information for this article comes from different materials in the Seneca County Historian's Office.

Chapter 14

185. *History of Seneca Co., New York.*
186. "Courthouse Complex Listed on National Register," *Interlaken (NY) Review*, January 20, 1977.

Chapter 15

187. "General History of the Music Trades of America," a manuscript in the Terwilliger Museum of the Waterloo Library and Historical Society.
188. Ibid.
189. Becker, *History of the Village of Waterloo*, 284.
190. Ibid., 298.
191. Ibid., 312.

192. "General History."
193. PublicResource.org, http://bulk.resource.org/courts/cF1/0134/001/00000357.txt; http://bulk.resource.org/courts.gov/c/F1/0134/001/00000354.txt.
194. "General History."
195. Becker, *History of the Village of Waterloo*, 331.
196. *Grip's Historical Souvenir of Waterloo*, 80.
197. Becker, *History of the Village of Waterloo*, 331.
198. Ibid., 403.

CHAPTER 16

199. Taken from the poster for the exhibition of the whale in Seneca Falls on November 10 and 11, 1891
200. Dick Case, "Memory Dredges Up a Whale of a Tale," *Post-Standard* (Syracuse, NY), February 21, 2012.
201. Poster information.
202. Becker, *History of the Village of Waterloo*, 86.
203. Poster information.
204. Ibid.
205. Case, "Memory Dredges Up a Whale of a Tale."
206. Becker, *History of the Village of Waterloo*, 86–87.
207. Case, "Memory Dredges Up a Whale of a Tale."
208. Dick Case, "An Overarching Need for Repair," *Post-Standard* (Syracuse, NY), April 5, 2012.

CHAPTER 18

209. Information taken from the genealogical index cards prepared by former Seneca County historian Betty Auten.
210. Ibid.
211. Astifan, "Dawn of Acknowledged Professionalism," 3–5.
212. *Rochester Union and Advertiser*, September 1, 1869, reprinted from the *Buffalo Express*.
213. Society for American Baseball Research, http://sabr.org.bioproj/person/26da490d.
214. Ibid.
215. *Clipper*, August 20, 1881.
216. Society for American Baseball Research, http://sabr.org.bioproj/person/26da490d.
217. Ibid.
218. *Clipper*, August 20, 1881.
219. Society for American Baseball Research, http://sabr.org.bioproj/person/26da490d.
220. *Clipper*, August 20, 1881.
221. Society for American Baseball Research, http://sabr.org.bioproj/person/26da490d.

222. Ibid.
223. DBpedia, http://dbpedia.org/page/Ezra_ Sutton.
224. Hall of Stats, http://www.hallofstats.com/articles/non-hall-of-fame-natinal-association-team.

CHAPTER 19

225. Digplanet, http://www.digplanet.com/wiki/Black_Diamond_(train).
226. Archer, *History of the Lehigh Valley Railroad*, 152.
227. Ibid.
228. My Large Scale, http://1stclass.mylargescale.com/scottychaos/BlackDiamondExpress/index.html.
229. Catskill Archive, http://www.catskillarchive.com/rrextra/lvblkdi.Html.
230. Lee, *History of Railroads in Tompkins County*, 41.
231. Archer, *History of the Lehigh Valley Railroad*, 152–53.
232. Catskill Archive, http://www.catskillarchive.com/rrextra/lvblkdi.Html.
233. Archer, *History of the Lehigh Valley Railroad*, 153.
234. Ibid., 243.
235. Ibid., 236.
236. Ibid., 266.
237. Ibid., 274.

CHAPTER 20

238. Wellman, *Road to Seneca Falls*, 131.
239. Ibid., 132.
240. Altschuler and Saltzbager, *Revivalism, Social Conscience and Community*, 34.
241. Wellman, *Road to Seneca Falls*, 116.
242. Ibid., 131–32.
243. Altschuler and Saltzbager, *Revivalism, Social Conscience and Community*, 96–97.
244. Jeremy Bement had been in a carriage-making business with partner Abraham Buckout. This business suffered greatly from the Panic of 1837. He joined the Presbyterian Church in 1839. Although he was characterized as conducting questionable business practices, he served on the village board of trustees in 1837 and again in 1846.
245. Daniel W. Forman was a lawyer and businessman. He had joined the Presbyterian Church in 1830 and became a ruling elder in 1832. He was the secretary of the Seneca County Anti-Slavery Society in 1839.
246. Dr. Joseph Kerr Brown was a physician and druggist. He had joined the Presbyterian Church in 1835 and was chosen a ruling elder in 1838. He was a village trustee in 1842 and 1843. He became president of the board in 1847. In 1849, he left Seneca Falls for Lockport, New York.
247. Altschuler and Saltzbager, *Revivalism, Social Conscience and Community*, 89.
248. Wellman, *Road to Seneca Falls*, 132.

249. Ibid., 132–33.
250. "Promiscuous" at this time meant any common public association/gathering of both females and males.
251. Wellman, *Road to Seneca Falls*, 133.
252. Altschuler and Saltzbager, *Revivalism, Social Conscience and Community*, 139.
253. Ibid.
254. Ibid., 140.
255. Wellman, *Road to Seneca Falls*, 133.
256. Altschuler and Saltzbager, *Revivalism, Social Conscience and Community*, 143.
257. Ibid., 20.
258. Ibid., 21.

Bibliography

Altschuler, Glenn C., and Jan M. Saltzbager. *Revivalism, Social Conscience and Community in the Burned-Over District: The Trial of Rhoda Bement*. Ithaca, NY: Cornell University Press, 1983.

Archer, Robert F. *The History of the Lehigh Valley Railroad: The Route of the Black Diamond*. Berkeley, CA: Howell-North Books, 1977.

Astifan, Priscilla. "The Dawn of Acknowledged Professionalism and Its Impact on Rochester Baseball." *Rochester History* 63 (Winter 2001).

Becker, John E. *A History of the Village of Waterloo, New York and Thesaurus of Related Facts*. Waterloo, NY: Waterloo Library and Historical Society, 1949.

Brown, John Howard. *The 20th Century Biographical Dictionary of Notable Americans*. New York: The Biographical Society, 1904.

Casstevens, David. "Ford Model T Full of Memories." *Finger Lakes (NY) Times*, October 5, 2008.

Delavan, Edith. *Landmarks of Seneca County: A Photographic Exploration of Historical Styles*. Ithaca, NY: Cayuga Press, 2004.

Doran, Robert E. *History of the Willard Hospital for the Insane: From Asylum to Drug Treatment Facility, Over 125 Years of Willard History*. Willard, NY: Willard Psychiatric Center, 1978.

Encyclopedia of New York State. Syracuse, NY: Syracuse University Press, 2005.

Freeman, Rich, and Sue Freeman. *Cobblestone Quest: Road Tours of New York's Historic Buildings*. Pine Glen Court, FL: Footprint Press, Inc., 2005.

Grip's Historical Souvenir of Seneca Falls, N.Y. Seneca Falls, NY: Seneca Falls Historical Society, 1991.

Grip's Historical Souvenir of Waterloo, N.Y. Waterloo, NY, 1903.

History of Seneca Co., New York with Illustrations Descriptive of Its Scenery, Palatial Residences, Public Buildings, Fine Blocks and Important Manufactories. Philadelphia: Everts, Ensign & Everts, 1876, 30–32.

King, Shelden S. *Trolleys to Cayuga Lake Park.* Seneca Falls, NY: Seneca Falls Historical Society, 1978.

Klees, Emerson. *More Legends and Stories of the Finger Lakes Region.* Rochester, NY: Friends of the Finger Lakes Publishing, 1997.

Lee, Hardy Campbell. *A History of Railroads in Tompkins County.* Ithaca, NY: Dewitt Historical Society of Tompkins County, 1947. Revised and expanded by Winton G. Rossiter and John Marcham. Ithaca, NY: The History Center of Tompkins County, 2008.

Merrill, Reverend Robert. "William Watts Folwell." *1906 Centennial Papers of the Seneca Falls Historical Society.*

Morrison, Wayne E., Sr. *New York State Agricultural College: A History.* Ovid, NY: W.E. Morrison & Co., 1978.

———. *Pictorial Album of the Willard Asylum, 1869–1886.* Reprint. Ovid, NY: 1978.

———. *Town & Village of Ovid, Seneca Co., N.Y.: An Early History.* Ovid, NY: W.E. Morrison, 1980.

Robinson, Elsie. *Sheldrake, 1789–1962.* Sheldrake-on-Cayuga, NY: self-published, 1962.

Rogers, A. Glenn. *Forgotten Stories of the Finger Lakes.* Geneva, NY: W.R. Carpenter, 1954.

Seneca County Historian's Office. *Discovering the Underground Railroad, Abolitionism and African American Life in Seneca County, New York, 1820–1880.* Seneca, NY: County of Seneca, 2006.

Shelgren, Olaf William, Jr., Cary Lattin and Robert W. Frasch. *Cobblestone Landmarks of New York State.* Syracuse, NY: Syracuse University Press, 1978.

Watrous, Hilda R. *The County Between the Lakes: A History of Seneca County, New York, 1876–1982.* Waterloo, NY: K-Mar Press, 1983.

Wellman, Judith. *Discovering the Underground Railroad, Abolitionism and African American Life in Seneca County, New York, 1820–1880.* Waterloo, NY: Seneca County Historian's Office, 2006.

———. *The Road to Seneca Falls: Elizabeth Cady Stanton and the First Woman's Rights Convention.* Chicago: University of Illinois Press, 2004.

Willers, Diedrich, Jr. *Centennial Historical Sketch of the Town of Fayette, Seneca County, New York 1800–1900.* Geneva, NY: W.F. Humphrey Press, 1900.

Index

G

H

I

J

K

L

M

N

O

P

R

S

T

V

W

About the Author

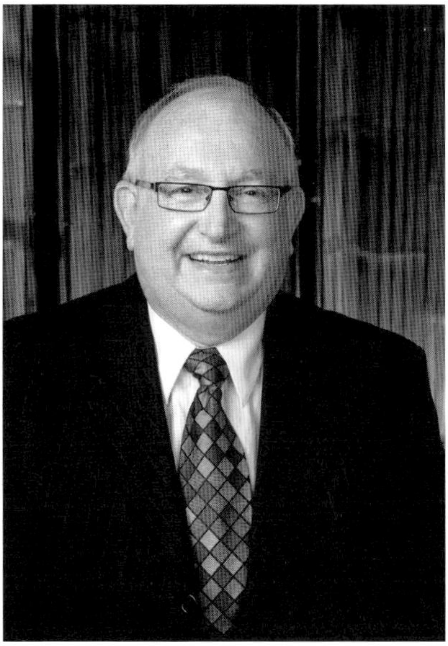

Walter Gable has been the Seneca County historian since August 2003. A lifelong resident of Seneca County, he is a graduate of the Romulus Central School District and earned his bachelor's and master's degrees at Syracuse University. His last thirty years of social studies teaching were at Mynderse Academy in the Seneca Falls Central School District. He was president of the New York State Council for the Social Studies (1997–98) and was recognized as its Distinguished Social Studies Educator in New York State in 2000. He received the Seneca Falls Community Service Award in 2013 and the Seneca County Chamber of Commerce's 2014 Lifetime Achievement Award. As the county historian, he writes local history articles on a monthly basis for two local newspapers and presents over forty programs a year to community and school groups. He credits his lifelong interest in history to the late Miss Ethel Buckley, his enthusiastic high school history teacher.